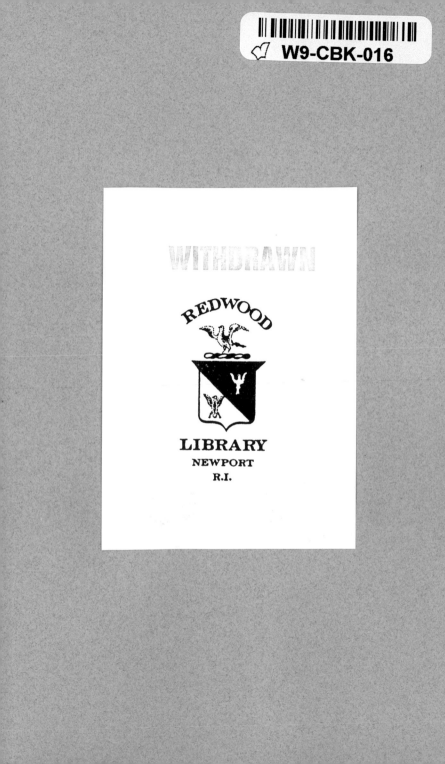

Music
of a
Distant
Drum

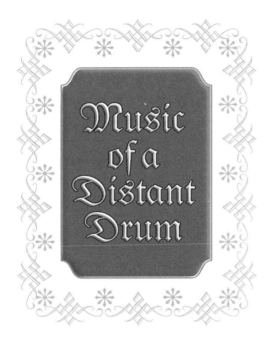

CLASSICAL ARABIC, PERSIAN,
TURKISH, AND HEBREW POEMS

Translated and Introduced by

Bernard Lewis

PRINCETON UNIVERSITY PRESS

PRINCETON AND OXFORD

Library of Congress Cataloging-in-Publication Data

Music of a distant drum : classical Arabic, Persian, Turkish, and Hebrew
poems / by Bernard Lewis.
p.   cm.
Selected Arabic, Hebrew, Persian, and Turkish poetry translated into English.
Includes bibliographical references.
ISBN 0-691-08928-0 (alk. paper)
1. Oriental poetry—Translations into English.   I. Lewis, Bernard.
PJ418 .M87   2001
808.81′0095—dc21   2001019858

British Library Cataloging-in-Publication Data is available

This book has been composed in Dante Typefaces
Printed on acid-free paper.⊗

www.pup.princeton.edu
Printed in the United States of America

3 5 7 9 10 8 6 4

CONTENTS

ACKNOWLEDGMENTS

MY THANKS are due to the librarians of the Topkapı Palace Museum in Istanbul and the Firestone Library at Princeton University, for their help in selecting and procuring illustrations; to Dr. Rachel Milstein for her invaluable advice in identifying and presenting them; to Professor Myriam Ayalon for kindly permitting me to use two pictures in her private possession, and, finally, to Mr. Jason Epstein, for planting and tending the seed which eventually germinated into this book.

Music
of a
Distant
Drum

A desert feast.

INTRODUCTION

SOME TWENTY-FIVE YEARS AGO I witnessed a remarkable
incident. The occasion was a lunch given by the late King
Hussein of Jordan for the chiefs of the loyal tribes. The
place was a group of tents in the eastern desert of the
kingdom; the principal guests were the tribal chiefs and
some of their tribesmen. The host was the late King, ac-
companied by his two brothers and their personal guests,
of whom I had the honor to be one (see photo opposite).
While the appropriate units of the royal Jordanian army
prepared the customary *mansif* feast of mutton and rice,
the King and his guests assembled in a large tent for the
usual exchange of compliments and pleasantries, with
appropriate refreshments. At a certain moment a tribal
poet appeared, with the traditional task of declaiming an
ode (*qasida*) in praise of the King. The ode, in appropri-
ately flowery literary Arabic, went on at considerable
length, and the King obediently sat cross-legged on his
carpet, occasionally nodding in appreciation. Then the
poet paused in his declamation. The King assumed that
he had finished, and began to rise to his feet with some
well-chosen words of thanks. But the poet had not
finished; he had merely paused for breath. Switching
abruptly from the classical Arabic of poetry to the collo-

quial Arabic of everyday speech he said to the King: "Wait a minute, I haven't finished yet." The King obediently resumed his seat and allowed the poet to complete his dithyramb.

This happened in a tent, not a palace; at a tribal rally, not a court ceremony. Even so, I find it difficult to conceive of any situation in any Western society, even the most democratic of republics and monarchies, in which a poet would feel free to put the head of state in his place in quite this way. This encounter between king and poet gave me a sharp and direct insight into something I knew only from literature and history—the love of poetry and respect for poets characteristic of Arab culture from antiquity to the present day. In classical times, we are told, the Arabs prized two arts above all others, and took pride in their mastery of both: poetry and eloquence. Both are arts of the word, and the immense esteem accorded to the word and to the skills and sciences associated with the word has remained a characteristic feature of Middle Eastern civilization. Poetry and poets in particular have been the subject of passionate, one might almost say obsessive, interest from the earliest times to the present day.

This respect for poets is the more remarkable if one compares it with the other arts. Music in medieval Middle Eastern society was widely appreciated, but musicians, even composers, were held in low esteem. Many of them were slaves, used by their wealthy or powerful owners to entertain their guests. Their names are known, if at all, only from literary mentions, and no method of preserving musical compositions was devised or borrowed

until the introduction of tablature and then of staff nota-
tion from Europe in the nineteenth century. Musicians
were entertainers, no more, and such reputation as they
acquired came principally from setting poems to music.

Artists, and especially architects, were slightly better
placed, but not by very much. They were seen basically
as artisans, working with their hands, and therefore of in-
ferior social status. The painting, as a separate work of art
to be hung on the wall, was unknown until modern
times, when it was introduced from Europe. Painters
were employed occasionally in the very early period and
again comparatively recently to do murals, but their
more usual and more characteristic task was to illustrate
manuscript books. The painter, like the musician, served
to embellish and offset the written or spoken word. What
little is known about artists, as about musicians, comes
from passing references or allusions. Metalworkers and
masons sometimes inscribed their names on their prod-
ucts, thus adding to our scanty knowledge. After the
Mongol conquests of the thirteenth century, perhaps be-
cause of Chinese influence, artists seem to have been held
in somewhat greater regard. More are known by name,
and for some we even have a few biographical details. Ar-
chitects in particular became better known since many of
them were military officers and as such enjoyed a certain
status in society. But for the most part artists and musi-
cians alike were not deemed worthy of the attention of
monarchs and ministers during their lifetime, nor of his-
torians after their death. It is not until the Ottoman pe-
riod that we have any detailed information—names,

biographies, etc.—and even then the information re-
mained sparse, until the processes of Westernization
brought Middle Eastern practice into line with that of the
Western world. The history of Islamic art and music and
the biographies of Islamic artists and musicians, with few
exceptions, were not written until Western orientalists
turned their attention to this aspect of Middle Eastern
culture and history.

All this is in striking contrast with the status of poetry
and poets. The Arabs developed an elaborate and sophis-
ticated literary analysis and literary history centuries be-
fore such studies were even conceived, let alone executed,
in Europe. The esteem, one might even say the cult, of
poets and poetry is the more remarkable and explains not
only the preservation of such vast quantities of poetry
but also of so much information about the poets, their
lives, and often, the circumstances in which particular
poems were composed and, so to speak, published. Even
caliphs and sultans did not disdain to compose and pub-
lish poems, on love (p. 48), on war (p. 150) and other
themes.

The place, the time, the people, the culture from
which these poems come are best defined by Islam. Its
heartlands are the region which in the twentieth century
came to be known as the Middle East, consisting of
Southwest Asia with extensions westward into North
Africa and eastward into Central Asia. For a while, it
stretched beyond North Africa into Spain, where for cen-
turies Islam was the dominant faith and Arabic the main
language of culture. In Asia it extended east and north of

Iran and Afghanistan into regions which historically, culturally, and ethnically form part of the traditional Middle East but were separated from it when these countries were conquered by the Russian czars and incorporated in the Russian empire. They were retained by the Soviets, and recovered their independence only with the collapse of the Soviet Union. In most of these regions the dominant languages are closely related to Turkish or Persian, and the dominant culture until the Russian conquest was that of Islam. They are now gradually resuming their historic links with the Islamic lands of the Middle East.

The time of this collection is also defined by Islam. The earliest poems come from the seventh century when the prophet Muhammad was born, lived, and died in Arabia, bringing a new scripture in Arabic and founding a new religion. The latest examples come from the eighteenth century, the final stage of classical Islamic literature, before poetry, like everything else, was transformed by the impact of the advancing and expanding civilization of the West.

Islam did not come into a new world but into a world of rich and ancient cultures, and some aspects of the civilization of classical Islam in its prime can be traced back to antiquity—to the heritage of Roman law and government, Greek science and philosophy, Judaeo-Christian religion and ethics, and beyond them to the more ancient civilizations of these lands. But Islamic civilization was nevertheless something new, distinctive and original, and in nothing is this more clearly seen than in its poetry.

The classical and scriptural language of Islam is of

course Arabic—the language of the Qur'an, of the oldest Islamic literature, of Muslim tradition and law. Structurally, Arabic ranks among the most ancient of the Semitic languages; historically, it is among the most recent. The name "Arab" is first attested in an Assyrian inscription of 853 B.C.E. Thereafter there are frequent references to Arabs, more precisely Arabians, in inscriptions, as well as in the later books of the Hebrew Bible and in Greek and Latin works. The oldest extant text in a language recognizable as Arabic was found in Namara, an oasis in the Syrian desert on the fringe of the Roman province of Arabia, and dated 223 of the Bosra era, corresponding to 328 C.E. Written in an Aramaic script but in the Arabic language, it records the death and celebrates the achievements of the famous Imru'l Qays, "King of all the Arabs." From the text of the inscription, it would seem that his kingship was over the nomads of northern and central Arabia.

Arabic first appears as a literary language in the seventh century C.E.—a newcomer among the ancient languages of the region, and it is to that comparatively recent time that the oldest Arabic poems are attributed, though some may contain verses of earlier origin. These Arabic poems have a character of their own, owing surprisingly little—far less than in law, science, philosophy, art, even religion—to the pre-Islamic cultures that were incorporated in the empire of the caliphs.

Three languages prevailed during the great age of Islamic civilization, though others were added later as Islam expanded into Asia, Africa and, for a while, Europe.

Of these, the first was Arabic, the language not only of religion but also of government and law, as well as of virtually every aspect of written culture. For some centuries, Arabic was in effect the sole written language of the Islamic world. Older languages survived for a while—Coptic among Christians, Hebrew among Jews, Aramaic among both—but these were in time restricted to ritual and literary use, and replaced by Arabic as the language of communication, both verbal and written.

A major exception was Iran where the Persians, though conquered and converted, nevertheless retained their own language and in time created a new form of that language. Persian, unlike Arabic, is not a Semitic language but belongs to the Indo-European family, which includes most of the languages of Europe as well as Sanskrit and its derivatives in India. The name "Iran" derives from the same root as the term "Aryan." The earliest Iranian inscriptions date from remote antiquity, and are in a script adapted from the Assyrian-Babylonian cuneiform. In the centuries immediately preceding the advent of Islam, the language of that time, which scholars sometimes call Middle Persian, was written in the so-called Pahlavi, based on the Aramaic script. The Zoroastrian scriptures are in this writing, and are still preserved among the Parsees, the Zoroastrians of the present day. The impact of the Arab conquest on the Persian language can be compared with the impact of the Norman conquest on Anglo-Saxon. The need to communicate led to a simplification of the grammar; the new order brought new classics and models and an immense new vocabulary, covering every aspect of intellectual, cultural, political, and social life. But Persian did not become Arabic; it became a new form of Persian, just as Anglo-Saxon became English, and with comparable richness, vigor, and flexibility.

A little later, the Turks were also brought into the Islamic fold, some by conquest, more by wandering missionaries. The name "Turk" is attested in both Byzantine and Chinese writings from the sixth century onward. Inscriptions and a small number of literary works in recognizably Turkic languages date from the seventh to the tenth centuries, and were written in a variety of scripts. After the conversion of almost all the Turkic peoples to Islam, they too adopted the Arabic script and many Arabic and also Persian words. In the vast area extending from western China to the Balkan peninsula, the Turks created more than one literary idiom. The best known of these is Ottoman Turkish, the language of the Ottoman Empire, from which is derived the language of the present-day Turkish Republic. Others include Azeri, the language of Azerbaijan, as well as several Central Asian literary languages. The poems in this collection are from the Ottoman and the closely-related Azeri literatures.

These new languages—Islamic Persian, Turkish, and later others—were written in Arabic script, which replaced the scripts previously used. These were retained, if at all, only in the rituals and sacred books of the pre-Islamic religions, now followed by ever dwindling minorities. The new, Islamized languages, along with an immense vocabulary of Arabic words, imported Arabic literary forms and, for a while, tastes. They also developed their own distinctive poetics. A notable development was in narrative, especially heroic narrative. The ancient Arabs had their heroic poetry, celebrating the deeds of the great warriors in the wars of pre-Islamic Arabia and in the early wars of Islam. Some later writings, such as an account of the life of Saladin in rhymed prose, have something of an epic quality. The Persians went a step further, creating an authentic epic tradition comparable with those of Greece, Rome, and the Vikings. This, too, became in time, a form of Persian national self-definition. The most famous of Persian epic poets, Firdawsi (940–1020), has been translated several times. An extract from the story of Farhad and Shirin, as told by the twelfth century Persian poet Nizami, exemplifies another form of narrative poetry (p. 117).

The addition of Hebrew deserves a note. Hebrew is a Semitic language, and as such is related to Arabic. But its cultural history is very different. Like Persian, it was already a written language in remote antiquity, and went through a number of phases of development, from the earlier to the later books of the Old Testament, through the vast rabbinical literature of the late pre-Christian and early Christian periods, and, particularly the creation of a rich and varied poetry of prayer. By the early centuries of the Christian era, Hebrew had ceased to be a spoken language, and Jews generally spoke the language of the country in which they lived, sometimes in a distinctive dialect of their own. A few passages in the Old Testament, and much of the rabbinic literature, are written in Aramaic, the most widely spoken language, or rather group of languages, in the countries of the Fertile Crescent until the Arab conquest and the subsequent Arabization of these lands. Jews in ancient Arabia spoke Arabic, and some of them composed poems which do not differ significantly from those of their pagan neighbors. Jews elsewhere, along with the rest of the population, gradually switched from Aramaic to Arabic.

But Hebrew, though no longer a vernacular, remained very much alive. As well as in worship, it was extensively used in scholarship, in literature, and even, to a remarkable extent, in business and private correspondence. Arabized Jews made an important contribution to Arabic literature, notably in science and philosophy. But for poetry—intimately linked with religion—they preferred to retain the Hebrew language, and to write it in the Hebrew script. Nevertheless, these Hebrew poems, written in the Middle East, North Africa, and Muslim Spain, are unmistakably part of the same cultural tradition as the Arabic, Persian, and Turkish poems produced in the realms of Islam. This Hebrew poetry reflects many aspects of Islamic literary culture, and even its language shows strong Arabic influence. We have become accustomed nowadays to speak in the Western world of a Judaeo-Christian tradition—a tradition which is predominantly Christian, but in which Jewish origins and later Jewish minorities play a significant part. One could with equal justification, and for similar reasons, speak of a Judaeo-Islamic tradition in the past, though no longer at the present time. The Hebrew poems translated here clearly belong to that tradition. Some Biblical figures, such as Joseph and Solomon (Arabic Yusuf and Sulayman), also figure prominently in Muslim stories and poetry.

How was a poem published, at a time when printing was unknown and even writing and reading were rare skills? The poet relied of course primarily on his own declamation of his poetry before a suitable audience, but from early times there were ways to supplement this, and a poet might employ one or more reciters known as *rawi*, whose task it was to memorize his poems and repeat them on suitable occasions to others, thus securing a wider circulation. The processes of memorizing and circulating the poem could of course be greatly facilitated and accelerated if the poem was set to music. In time, the *rawi* became a kind of professional performer, reciting poems before an audience. The Arab literary historians tell many stories of this or that *rawi* —his extraordinary memory, his enormous repertoire, his entrancing performance. One *rawi* is credited with having recited 2,900 poems at a single sitting. Sometimes the *rawi* was himself an apprentice or aspiring poet, trying to gain a hearing for his own compositions. Such *rawis* were suspected of editing or even inventing some of the verses they declaimed in the names of the great masters of the past. These accusations raised serious questions concerning the accuracy and even the authenticity of the poems that were transmitted in this way. It was perhaps for this reason that among the Persians and Turks it became common practice for the poet to incorporate his signature in the poem.

For the first century or more of the Islamic era, Arabic

poems were transmitted orally, and this oral transmission adds to the problems of accuracy and authenticity. Verses appear in variant versions, and are attributed to different poets. Some are palpably projections backward of later attitudes and events. From an early date the Arabs developed a scholarly discipline to study and, where possible, to answer such questions. This study used several methods—philological, historical, and literary. The Arab scholars of the Middle Ages made a great effort to establish and authenticate texts, though many problems remained to which modern scholarship has sometimes given conflicting answers. Some time in the eighth century—the second of Islam—an unknown *rawi* compiled the famous collection known as the *Muᶜallaqat,* literally the hanging or suspended poems, a collection of poems each by a different poet of the pre-Islamic era, each regarded as its creator's masterpiece. This collection was followed by many others, some of them anthologies, grouped in variously defined categories, some of them the collected poems of a single poet. Such a collection was known as a *diwan* (Persian and Turkish *divan*), a term that has been retained until modern times.

Sometimes the compilers of anthologies added some explanatory notes and commentaries. This in turn developed into two new literary genres: poetics, a science inherited from classical antiquity, and literary history. An early example of the first was a work by Ibn al-Muᶜtazz (d. 908), a prince of the caliphal ᶜAbbasid family and himself a poet of distinction. A better known treatise is that of Ibn Qutayba (d. 889), who wrote a famous work entitled *The Book of Poetry and Poets* and also compiled a literary thesaurus in ten books. The most esteemed and most informative work of classical literary history is the *Kitab al-Aghani*, the *Book of Songs*, by Abu'l-Faraj al-Isfahani (d. 967), as his name indicates, a native of Isfahan in Iran. In twenty-one volumes, Abu'l-Faraj provides an invaluable store of information concerning the biographies of poets and musicians, with samples of their work and details of the circumstances of their composition.

Many other works on poetics and literary history followed, in every age and in every land where the Arab language and its literature flourished. Later, as new Persian and Turkish literatures developed under Arab-Islamic influence, a similar scholarly literature was produced in these languages.

A notable feature of this literature was the collections of biographies of poets, first in Arabic, later more extensively in Persian and Turkish. While often anecdotal and sometimes of questionable accuracy, these collected biographies form an immensely rich source of information both on the development and on the perception of poetry in these cultures. They also form the starting point and basis of much modern scholarship.

Arabic poets devised and used elaborate rules of prosody, expressed in a number of different verse forms designed for a variety of purposes. These were adopted and often modified by the Persians and the Turks, who added new forms of their own. Certainly the best known of these among Western readers is the quatrain, *ruba'i,* plural *ruba'iyyat,* made famous in the Western world by Fitzgerald's translation of ʿOmar Khayyam. Similar forms were also adopted in other languages. To give the reader some idea of the rhythms and tonalities in the original, I have appended the texts of four quatrains, one from each of the four languages (see Appendix). The Turkish poem is given in the standard modern Turkish orthography, which replaced the Arabic script in 1928; the other three are transcribed, two from the Arabic, one from the Hebrew script. According to a thirteenth century treatise on Persian prosody, the *rubaʿi* was invented by an ancient poet who heard a child cry out during a ball game, "The ball is rolling, rolling to the bottom of the hole" in rhyme and quantitative meter. Rhyme is indeed an important feature of Arabic poetry and of others under Arabic influence. This is in striking contrast with Latin, Greek, and Biblical Hebrew alike.

Poets gained their livelihood in various ways. In the earliest tribal societies, a poet was a member of a tribe, more specifically of a family within the tribe. His status was determined by the status of his family. In the more complex life of the cities, we find poets at various economic and social levels. Some were themselves men of wealth or power or both, and had no need of gainful employment. Many belonged to the learned professions—teaching and religion, to which one might add service in the state secretariat. Some were of relatively humble origin. We hear, for example, of a saddler's apprentice, a small storekeeper, a carpenter, and the like. A special category consisted of those who were designated by the Persian word *rind*, defined by the dictionary as a knave, a rogue, a drunkard, a debauchee, a vagabond. The term was taken up by Persian and later Turkish poets and especially by mystics and given a positive connotation. In this sense, it denotes the mystic who has abandoned all ambition and all self-interest in contrast with the insincerity and selfishness of the formally pious, even—and perhaps especially—of the ascetic. The term was frequently used by Hafiz and was also later applied to him.

Like their counterparts in the West, poets in the Middle East depended heavily on patronage for their support, on protection and funding from kings, princes, and other men of wealth and power. They were expected to earn their keep by composing and declaiming poems in praise of their patrons, and panegyric poetry became a profession, even a vocation. Many tales are told of relations between poets and patrons and of rivalries between poets for the attention of this or that munificent benefactor. One such tale, almost certainly apocryphal, is told of the Persian poet Amir Muʿizzi, (d. ca. 1125–7) who was chief court poet to the Seljuq Sultan Sanjar. Determined to keep his position, he denounced every rival as a plagiarist and claimed that the poems which they recited to the Sultan as their own had in fact been copied, through reciters, from his work. This method was successful in preserving Muʿizzi's monopoly until the aspiring young poet Anvari (d. ? 1191) found a way of circumventing it. Dressing himself in rough peasant clothes and assuming an appearance of ignorance and stupidity, he presented himself to Muʿizzi and told him that he had composed a very beautiful panegyric. He then recited the opening verses, which didn't scan and conveyed no meaning. Muʿizzi saw in this an opportunity to amuse the court and at the same time stress his own superiority. The following day he presented Anvari to the Sultan, saying "Here is one who wishes to recite an ode that he has composed in your honor." Anvari then threw aside his disguise and declaimed a truly magnificent ode of praise, to the delight of the Sultan and the discomfiture of Muʿizzi. Anvari became famous, and is regarded as one of the great masters of panegyric poetry in Persian. Later, when he fell from grace and was banished from the court, he composed some poems denouncing the venality and insincerity of court poetry and the sycophancy of its practitioners. "It is better" he says "for you to earn your bread as a scavenger rather than as a poet." In another poem he even speaks of poetry as "male menstruation."

Some other poets speak light-heartedly or even disrespectfully of their art and even of their patrons. The twelfth-century Spanish Arab poet Ibn Quzman, with charming irony, begins a poem by describing his dalliance with his mistress and ends as he explains to her that he must go off to earn his living by praising his generous patron. The Spanish Hebrew poet al-Harizi denounces and even threatens a patron—presumably a private individual—whose gifts did not come up to his expectations (p. 196). These were no idle threats. The great Arab poet al-Mutanabbi worked for a while as court panegyrist to the Nubian eunuch Kafur who was the de facto ruler of Egypt in the mid-tenth century. Later he turned against his former patron, and denounced him in a series of biting satires.

But most panegyric poets seem to have been well satisfied with their profession, and one of them, the Persian poet Farrukhi, in a striking metaphor, describes how he came like a merchant from his native Sistan, bringing uniquely precious merchandise—the word, the tongue, and his poetic gift. Patrons did not limit their generosity to payment for panegyrics. There are many tales of royal bounty to poets, especially for epic and other narrative poems. But panegyric remained a primary function.

One of the most important functions of poets and poetry in traditional society was what we nowadays call propaganda, or as some prefer to call it, public relations. In the days before journalists, propagandists, public relations men, and spin doctors, poets were often called upon to fulfill these functions. They were, in many ways, the public relations consultants of chiefs and of rulers, and had been engaged in these tasks for a very long time. The Roman emperor Augustus, for example, had his court poets in Rome, doing PR work for the empire in general and the emperor in particular. One might even argue that Virgil's great epic, the *Aeneid,* is in part a public relations exercise for the Roman imperial idea.

This aspect of classical Arab poetry is familiar to all students of Arabic literature. The traditional classification by the Arab literary historians of the different types of poetry includes at least three that have an important element of propaganda: the *fakhr,* or boast, in which the poet makes propaganda on behalf of himself and his tribe; the *madih,* or panegyric, in which he promotes his ruler or patron, and the *hija²,* usually translated satire, consisting of invective and ridicule against hostile or rival groups or persons. A form combining elements of the *fakhr* and the *madih* is the elegy, the lament for the dead. Some of these, notably the poems of al-Khansaʾ, reflect deep personal feeling. Others share the courtly and formal character of the panegyric.

In its earliest and simplest form, as described by the Arab literary historians, the *fakhr* is a technique of battlefield propaganda, designed to strengthen the morale of one's own fighters while undermining that of the enemy. It thus corresponds, in some ways, to the epics and sagas and heroic ballads of other cultures. An early Arabic translation of Aristotle's *Poetics* somewhat improbably identifies *hijaʾ* with comedy and *madih* with tragedy. In Persian and Turkish especially, *hijaʾ* is often blended with humor. Indeed, humor is a distinctive feature of classical Middle Eastern poetry, ranging from the pungent epigram (e.g., p. 116) to the good-humored sally, evoking an appreciative smile (e.g., p. 101). An early example is the Persian poet Rudagi's gently ironic poem, comparing the rewards of serving God and serving the king (p. 91).

In the earliest Arabic poetry, the rivalries and conflicts reflected are usually personal or tribal. Later, in the Islamic empire, the differences become more complex, and there are poems illustrating the tensions between rival groups. Sometimes these are simply political, between rival contenders for power; sometimes religious, between the followers of different religious teachers or teachings; sometimes ethnic or even racial, as for example in the poetic wars between Persians and Arabs, or between blacks and whites. In the vast, multi-racial empire of the caliphs, such rivalries were inevitable, and they gave rise to a considerable literature ranging from good-humored banter to embittered hostility. The poems translated here include examples of two such conflicts. One group (pp. 39–41 and pp. 44–46) comes from black slaves, some enslaved and imported from Africa, some born in captivity. Like their counterparts elsewhere, they learned and mastered the language of their owners, and used it to good effect. A group of black poets in the seventh and eighth centuries, known as "the Crows of the Arabs," is particularly famous. Another form of ethnic self-assertion was that of the Persians. After the conquest of Iran by the Muslim Arabs in the seventh century, the old Persian empire was extinguished and the followers of the old Persian religion dwindled into a minority. But the Persian spirit smoldered on, and in time the Persian poets began to reassert themselves against Arab domination, at first in Arabic, later in Persian. An Arabic poem by the eleventh-century poet Mihyar al-Daylami, from Daylam, the Persian province immediately south of the Caspian Sea, is a fine example of both Arab verse and Persian pride (p. 70). There are many others.

Poetry came to play an important, indeed a central and essential part in Persian identity and self-awareness. While Persians, Arabs, and Turks were all Muslims, the quality of their Islam and the artistic and other expression that they gave to it developed significant differences. Some have likened the split between the different

branches of Islam to the conflicts in Christendom be-
tween Orthodox and Catholic, between Catholic and
Protestant. In theological terms such a comparison is
meaningless. Islam has so far known neither schism nor
reformation, and the strictly theological differences be-
tween Shiʿa and Sunni Islam are relatively unimportant.
The question of ecclesiastical jurisdiction, so important
in Christendom, simply did not arise in a society which,
until modern times, had created no ecclesiastical institu-
tions, and where the distinctively Christian differentiation
between state and church, God and Caesar, was mean-
ingless. But the cultural differences were enormous, and
in terms of their magnitude though not of their content,
one might not unjustly compare the differences between
Arab, Persian, and Turkish Islam with the differences be-
tween northern Protestantism, southern Catholicism,
and eastern Orthodoxy in European Christendom.

Poets seem at times to have played a part in some of
the wars and conflicts of early Islamic history, as propa-
gandists on behalf of one or another individual or fac-
tion. There are episodes in the biography of the Prophet
in which different poets appear among both his support-
ers and his opponents. From the narrative it is clear that
their propaganda efforts, on both sides, were considered
important if not decisive. The Umayyad Caliphs, and
thereafter virtually all Muslim rulers, had court poets.
In the days before printing and modern methods of
communication, poetry had obvious advantages. Poems
could be memorized, recited, and often sung, thus reach-
ing a very wide audience.

It was not only rulers who employed poets in this way. They were also used by rebels and sectarian leaders to disseminate seditious propaganda, and sometimes even for purely personal ends. As well as rulers, private individuals also employed poetic spokesmen, to project a favorable image, or even to sell a commodity. The *Kitab al-Aghani* tells a story of a merchant who went from Iraq to Medina in Arabia with a collection of ladies' veils of various colors. He managed to sell all but the black ones, which were left on his hands. He complained of this to his friend the poet al-Darimi, who had recently renounced music and poetry and taken up the ascetic life. Darimi said to the merchant: "Don't worry. I shall get rid of them for you; you will sell the whole lot." The poet then composed these verses:

> Go ask the one in the black veil.
> What have you done to a devout ascetic?
> He had already girded up his garments for prayer
> until you appeared to him at the door of the mosque.

This, says the author of the *Kitab al-Aghani,* was set to music and became very popular: "People said, 'Darimi is at it again and has given up his asceticism.' There was not a lady of refinement in Medina who did not buy a black veil, and the Iraqi merchant sold all he had."[1] And so, behind a black veil, the singing commercial was born. Poetry was also used for what we would nowadays call the social column, as a way of announcing births, deaths,

[1] Abu'l-Faraj al-Isfahani, *Kitab al-Aghani,* vol. iii, (Cairo 1347 / 1929), pp. 45–46.

marriages, and other events of this kind. The hunt—a social occasion, a popular pastime, a training for war—inspired an entire poetic genre.

In addition to the public poetry, there is of course also personal poetry expressing personal feelings and attitudes, venting personal problems. In Middle Eastern as in other literatures, many poems are devoted to wine, women, and song. These raise interesting questions in a religious society where wine is strictly forbidden and access to women is subject to a whole series of religious, social, and legal constraints.

Despite the Muslim ban on wine, there are innumerable poems by ostensibly Muslim poets celebrating its delights and its effects. The convention, adopted at an early date, that wine was a metaphor for divine love and drunkenness a metaphor for ecstasy helped to provide some cover. The same metaphor was also used, less convincingly, for physical love, seen as representing mystical union with God. Sexual activity outside the strict limits laid down by the holy law was a sin and a crime, and could incur severe punishment.

Nevertheless, there is a rich literature of love poetry, expressing sentiments, relationships, and aspirations both inside and outside the law. The poems reflect a wide variety of approaches and activities, in changing times and different places, from the pagan desert to the Muslim city. They present the lover in many roles, from the boastful prowler and philanderer to the chaste and submissive adorer-from-afar. The stricter moral codes enforced by Islam brought a new respect for chastity, and a consequent spread of the pangs of unfulfilled love. A recurring theme is that of the parting of lovers, sometimes at dawn after a nocturnal assignation, sometimes because of the migrations of their tribes. An unusual farewell is that of the pre-Islamic Arab poet al-Aʿsha in the poem I have entitled "Bill of Divorcement" (p. 37). The early commentators offer various explanations of the circumstances in which this poem was composed.

Much of the poetry comes from cities and more specifically from royal courts, very different from the relative freedom of pre-Islamic and early Islamic times. The free lady, so important in early poetry, disappears, and the well-guarded harem makes the nocturnal assignation dangerous if not impossible. Often, the woman addressed in love poetry is a slave, perhaps one of the educated and cultivated singing girls who provided the feminine element in court society and are celebrated by many writers. The great essayist and litterateur ʿAmr ibn Bahr al-Jahiz (776–869), by common consent one of the great classical masters of Arabic prose, even devoted a whole essay to the subject of singing girls which has been admirably translated into English.[2]

In the Islamic world as in the pre-modern West, the poets were overwhelmingly male. For the most part, women had no access either to the education which would have enabled them to develop a poetic talent or to the patronage which would have enabled them to exercise it. In a society in which women were excluded from

[2]*The Epistle on Singing Girls of Jahiz,* edited with translation and commentary by A.F.L. Beeston, (Warminster, 1980).

public life and secluded in the home, there was little op-
portunity for them to find a place in the world of poets
and of poetry. But there are exceptions. One such was
Khansaʾ (d. ca. 640), one of the very few women poets
whose poems were actually collected in a *divan*. Her best
known works are her elegies on her two brothers and
four sons, all killed in battle. Another is Rabiʿa (d. 801),
known for her religious poetry. A Turkish example is
Mihri Hatun or Lady Mihri (d. 1506, pp. 151–52).

The different literary situation of men and women is
vividly illustrated in the most famous of all Middle East-
ern romances, that of Majnun and Layla. Majnun, liter-
ally, possessed by a jinni, that is to say, demented, was the
name given to a young Bedouin, purportedly in the early
days of Islam, who fell madly in love with a young
Bedouin woman called Layla. In some versions she was a
cousin whom he had known as a child; in others a
stranger whom he met by chance. Majnun asked for her
in marriage. But Layla's father had made arrangements
to assign her to another man and she was therefore not
available for Majnun. In the romance, Majnun suffers the
pangs of unrequited, unconsummated love, and eventu-
ally dies of his suffering. There are many narrative
poems telling the romance of Majnun and Layla, in Ara-
bic, Persian, Turkish, and other languages, and great
numbers of Arabic poems attributed to Majnun himself,
telling of his love for Layla and bewailing his unhappy
lot. The difference in status between the two of them is
vividly exemplified in one of the very few poems attrib-
uted to Layla.

There is nothing Majnun endured for love
That I did not endure as he did.
But he proclaimed love's secret
While I hid it, pining away . . .

There was a time when the word "gender" had a pri-
marily grammatical meaning, and was used to denote a
difference between words rather than between people. It
still retains some importance in this sense, especially—
since languages may vary in the perception and expres-
sion of gender differences—for the translator of poetry.
Arabic and Hebrew, like English, use different words for
"he" and "she," but have no word for "it." They have only
two genders, masculine and feminine, and no neuter. The
personal pronoun "you," in both the singular and plural
forms, must be masculine or feminine—a matter of some
importance in poetry. Even the verb, in some though not
all tenses and persons, is modified for gender, depending
on whether the subject is masculine or feminine. Persian
and Turkish go to the opposite extreme and do not reflect
gender at all; not in the verb, not even in personal pro-
nouns. In both languages "he," "she," and "it" are the
same word. This sometimes poses problems for the trans-
lator. For example, in Saʿdi's poem "The Moth and the
Candle" (p. 125), the English "it" seemed inappropriate,
and I took the liberty of making the moth and the candle,
respectively, masculine and feminine. The image of the
moth and the candle is also used by other poets.

This lack of grammatical gender may give rise to a
sometimes useful ambiguity in love poetry, where the ob-

ject of the poet's passion may be variously understood as male, female, or divine. Homosexuality is condemned and forbidden by the holy law of Islam, but there are times and places in Islamic history when the ban on homosexual love seems no stronger than the ban on adultery in, for example, Renaissance Italy or seventeenth-century France. Some poems are openly homosexual; some poets, in their collected poems, even have separate sections for love poems addressed to males and females. Erotic imagery was also used to express religious sentiments, especially but not exclusively in mystical poetry. The assigning of religious meanings to apparently erotic poetry is familiar to us from other cultures, notably from the Biblical book of the Song of Songs.

Religious poetry has a special place in Islamic literature There are no hymns or fugues in Islamic worship, only the simple recitation or cantillation of verses from the Qurʾan. There was therefore no development of liturgical poetry such as we find in Christianity and in Judaism. But religious poetry enters Islam by another route—the way of the Sufi. The name is said to come from an Arabic word meaning wool, denoting the simple and unadorned dress of mystics and ascetics. The word was applied at an early stage to those Muslims who, like some Jews and Christians before them, wanted to go beyond the simple observance of religious rules and practices as prescribed by the faith, and to achieve mystical experience, harmonizing ritual with ecstasy. The wearing of rough, simple garments was in a sense a reaction against the increasingly luxurious attire of an increasingly affluent society.

The Sufi found many ways of reaching toward mystical union with God; through poetry, through music, even—reviving an ancient tradition—through the dance, as exemplified in the rituals of the so-called dancing and whirling dervishes. Poetry played an important part in the Sufi's search for mystical experience, and even in religious rituals, notably in the dervish fraternities. The first Sufi poems are in Arabic, the language of Islamic scripture, law, and prayer. In the eleventh century, Persian and later Turkish Sufis began to compose mystical poetry in their own languages. Sufi poems in this collection include those of the poetess Rabiʿa, Al-Hallaj, and Ibn al-ʿArabi in Arabic; Galib and Nesimi in Turkish; and of course the great Persian masters, Hafiz and Rumi.

The imagery of love and wine—of passion and intoxication—provided the means to express the love of God and the mystical experience of union with Him. Not surprisingly, the dividing line between sexual and allegorical love is sometimes problematic and the poets who celebrate them have at times been regarded with a certain suspicion. Sufi poets often went dangerously near the limits of orthodoxy, expressing ideas which in other times and places might be called pantheist or even relativist, as for example in some of the poems of Rumi. Some of the less fortunate Sufi poets paid a high price for these deviations from strict orthodox teaching.

It is always difficult to translate works of literature, especially poetry. The difficulty is incomparably greater when one is translating works not just from another language but from another civilization.[3] An example occurs in the last line of a poem by ʿUmar ibn al-Farid (p. 77) which begins with the words "your reward." The Arabic is *haqq,* a word with a wide range of connotations and associations, depending on context. Its primary meaning is truth; it can also connote rightness, what is just and proper, and, in certain contexts, what is incumbent or obligatory. In modern Arabic *haqq,* plural *huquq,* is the common word for rights, as in "rights of man," "civil rights," and so on. Yet to speak of "your right" in a translation of a medieval mystical poem seems to me misleading. I can think of no precise English equivalent for this Arab-Islamic compound of authenticity, appropriateness, and justice. "Reward" seemed to me the closest to the meaning and intention of the original.

The poetry of the Middle East comes from a world nurtured on different scriptures and classics, shaped and inspired by different history and memories, in which words not only have different meanings, which is normal, but different ranges of meaning, so that the simple listing of equivalents that we find in a dictionary can be dangerously misleading. Each civilization has its own universe of discourse, its own framework of allusion and reference, readily understood by those to whom it is addressed, and unintelligible or even invisible to others. A passing reference in an Arabic poem may bring immedi-

[3]For a fuller discussion of these problems, see my "Translation from Arabic," in *Proceedings of the American Philosophical Society,* 24 / 1, February 1980, pp. 41–47, reprinted in Bernard Lewis, *Islam and the West,* (Oxford: New York, 1993), pp. 61–71.

ate understanding and emotional response to an Arab, or even to a classically educated Persian or Turk, but it would need heavy footnoting to make it intelligible to a Western reader. It is not only the semantics that are different. The differences go far deeper, sometimes reaching to the very roots of human emotion, experience, and thought.

A particularly difficult problem in what one might call intercultural translation is that of images. Some refer to basic human qualities, and can be readily recognized and understood even between remote and unrelated peoples. Others may be unintelligible or even grotesque. For example, the image of the heart as the seat of the emotions is common to many cultures, including those of both the Western and Islamic worlds. But in Arabic and Persian and some other languages, the liver, as well as the heart, sometimes serves the same purpose. This occurs occasionally in Latin poetry, but in modern English it would strike most readers as comic or absurd. Usually, the translator may replace "liver" by the more familiar "heart" without too much disservice to the original. But sometimes this simple solution is not possible, as for example, in some lines from the late fourteenth- to early fifteenth-century Turkish poet Şeyhi:

> Heart, do not die of parting, for
>   the breath of resurrection is coming.
> Liver, do not burn with grief, for
>   succor is coming.

Şeyhi, it may be noted, was a physician by profession. I remember many years ago being given a piece of excellent advice by a great master of translation, the late Arthur Waley, justly admired for his magnificent translations from Chinese and Japanese. He would, he said, lay down only one firm rule for translators: never introduce an image which is not in the original. If you can use the original image in English, well and good. If you can't, leave it out, and don't try to replace it by some equivalent. It won't work. I have followed this rule. I cannot claim to have rendered into English everything that is in the original—such a feat would be beyond my powers—but I have tried not to introduce anything in the translation that is not in the original. This precluded any attempt that I might have made to translate these poems into rhymed and metric English verse, a task which would inevitably have required the insertion of new material. Instead, I have sought to convey as much as I can of the poetry of the original in poetic and rhythmic English prose.

Some of these translations of poetry were made during the war, that is, more than half a century ago. As every survivor will recall, in wartime there are long periods of intense boredom, when nothing much changes, and there is nothing one can do. Like so many others, I usually carried a little book in my pocket, to read when circumstances permitted. I preferred poetry, not only for its own sake, but also—perhaps more especially—because it offered more reading time in relation to weight and bulk than prose. Later, I found that the ratio could be still further improved by reading poetry in a foreign language. It also required greater concentration—of some advantage in excluding such distractions as exploding bombs and shells.

At some stage I found that I could tilt the balance still further in my favor and dispense with the book entirely by learning a few poems by heart and then trying to translate them into English. Memorizing poetry was child's play—literally, since as children at school in England we were required to memorize vast quantities. Translation was of course more difficult, but there too, tools acquired in dealing with Virgil and Horace were honed on both ancient and modern poets of the Middle East. During the past half century, in the course of my work as a historian, I read many of these poets, and from time to time felt the urge to try my hand at rendering them into English. A poem is a historical document, no less than a treaty, an inscription, or a chronicle, especially in a society in which poets and poetry are held in such high regard and play so significant a role in public life. Reading them may contribute to historical understanding as well as—and sometimes more than—to aesthetic appreciation.

In choosing poems for translation and translations for inclusion, I was guided by certain criteria. The first is quality, or to put it differently, that I liked it. The second is translatability, meaning that I felt I could translate it into intelligible English, able to stand on its own without needing any elaborate scholarly apparatus. An occasional brief explanatory note here and there might be acceptable, but an extensive critical apparatus would destroy the whole purpose of the work. A further requirement is that at least some of the poems should be in some way illustrative of the time and place from which they derive and should exemplify some aspect of its history and culture.

And again, that aspect should be intelligible and recognizable, without elaborate explanations and annotations, to the reader of our own time.

An important consideration was of course whether poems were already available in English translation. In a few places, I have indulged myself by including my versions of poems which I later discovered had already been published in English translation. There is no reason why the reader should not have more than one translation of a fine poem at his disposal, especially if the translators come from different times and places. But in general I have tried to avoid duplication and to confine myself to poems of which my translation, as far as I am aware, is the first to appear in English. These criteria required the exclusion of many of the most original, most important, most esteemed, and to put it simply, the best poems from these literatures. It is therefore only in the most general sense that I can claim that this collection of translations is in any way representative of the cultures of the time, the place, the nations, or even of the individual poets from which they come. A truly representative selection would raise difficult, perhaps insuperable, problems of translation and communication.

There are many statements by Arab and other authors on the role and the importance of poetry in society. The point is well made by the ninth-century Arab author Ibn Qutayba, in his book on literature:

> Poetry is the mine of knowledge of the Arabs, the book of their wisdom, the muster roll of their history,

the repository of their great days, the rampart protecting their heritage, the trench defending their glories, the truthful witness on the day of dispute, the final proof at the time of argument. Whoever among them can bring no verse to confirm his own nobility and the generous qualities and honored deeds which he claims for his forebears, his endeavors are lost though they be famous, effaced by the passage of time though they be mighty. But he who binds them with rhymed verse, knots them with scansion, and makes them famous through a rare line, a phrase grown proverbial, a well-turned thought, has made them eternal against time, preserved them from negation, averted the plot of the enemy, and lowered the eye of the envious.[4]

[4]Ibn Qutayba, Abu Muhammad ʿAbdallah, ʿUyun al-Akhbar, 4 vols., ed. Ahmad Zaki al-ʿAdawi, (Cairo 1343–8 / 1925–30), vol. ii. p. 185.

Arabic
Poems

Bill of Divorcement

Go, my friend, you are free.
Such is the human lot, by day or night
Leave me, for leaving is better than the rod
that would have hung, threatening, over your head.
Not because you have committed any grave offense
nor brought us any dire calamity—
Leave blameless and chaste,
loving and loved.
Taste some other man, and I
shall taste another, just as you will.

Al-A͑sha

Elegy

Shed tears in plenty, eyes, and let them not congeal.
Do you not weep the bold, the steadfast?
Do you not weep for Sakhr the generous,
he of the lofty tent, the long baldrick
who led his tribe before he grew a beard?
When men stretched out their hands
in battle, in quest of honor
competing to excel—he came, stretched out a hand,
and reached the glory that was beyond their reach.
He brought them what raised them up
though he was the youngest of them in years.

Al-Khansa'

She points with her comb and says to her companion,
"Is that the slave of Banu'l-Hashas, the slick rhymster?"
She saw a threadbare saddlebag, a worn cloak,
a naked negro such as men own.
These girls excite other men and turn away from my
    shock of hair,
despising me as I can clearly see.
If I were pink of color, these women would love me
but my Lord has shamed me with blackness.
Yet it does not diminish me that my mother was a slave-
    woman
who tended the udders of she-camels.

Suhaym

If you imprison me, you imprison the son of a slave-
    woman,
  if you free me, you free a tawny lion.
Prison is no more than the shadow of the house where I
    live,
  and a whipping no more than hide meeting hide.

Suhaym

Though I hate slavery, I would gladly serve
  as camelherd to Ibn Ayman
provided that I am not sold, and that they tell me,
    "Slave! Take the maiden her evening drink!"
And I may prop a languorous lady, sleep stripping her
      garment, baring her breast, for even a slave may
        find an assignation.
And if she refuse me, I hold her tight, she cannot break
      free, so that her beauty and her sweetness are
        manifest.

Suhaym

She said: "Do not loiter by our house,
　　my father is a jealous man."
I said: "I seek the best he has,
　　my sword is sharp and keen."
She said: "The castle is between us."
　　I said: "I shall climb over it."
She said: "The sea lies between us."
　　I said: "I am a skillful swimmer."
She said: "Seven brothers stand about me."
　　I said: "I am mighty and invincible."
She said: "A lion crouches between us."
　　I said: "I am a rampant lion."
She said: "God is above us."
　　I said: "My Lord is merciful and forgiving."
She said: "You have out-argued me.
　　Come when the evening company sleeps
And fall on me as the dew falls
　　by night, when none forbids or interferes."

Waddah al-Yaman

I reached for her and she swayed towards me
like a bough moved by the breeze.
After a quarrel she let me taste her sweetness
like honey mixed with pure wine
and then her body like a shirt touched
the skin of her suffering, passionate lover.
Panting, she complained that her sash was tight
and cast off her veil towards me.
I liked it when she drew back her hands
in the sleeves of her shift to loosen her sash.
Then she said when the glow of dawn appeared
shedding light on any who looked,
"My cousin, let my soul be your ransom. I fear
lest some secret enemy speak and do us wrong."

ʿUmar ibn Abi Rabiʿa

I remember how I stayed the night of al-Bab, grasping
   the hand of a houri-eyed one like the moon
and, swept by my uncontained passion for her,
   I seemed to fly, and my tears streamed on my breast.
Oh, could I but spend a night again
   like that night of ours, until I see the gleam of dawn,
I would amuse her with talk, and sometimes
   she would amuse me with kisses from her lips.
If God would but ordain one more such night,
   then would my Lord know how great is my thankfulness.

Nusayb ibn Rabah

Blackness does not diminish me, as long
as I have this tongue and a stout heart.
Some are raised up by their lineage;
the verses of my poems are my lineage.
How much better is a black, eloquent and keen-minded,
than a mute white.
The nobleman envies me from his heights
for this merit, and no one gloats over me.

Nusayb ibn Rabah

If I am jet-black, musk is blacker,
and there is no medicine for the blackness of my skin.
I have a nobility that towers over their depravity
like the sky over the earth.
There are few of my like among your menfolk;
there is no lack of your kind among the women.
If you accept my advances, you respond to one who is
    compliant
if you refuse, then we are equal.

Nusayb ibn Rabah

I obeyed you, Iblis,* for seventy years, but now I am
    old, my time has come,
I flee to God, certain that I must encounter death.
For a long time Iblis, the father of the genies, let my
    camel trot without bridle,
He tempted me to ride it, bestriding it sometimes
    before me, sometimes behind me,
and he told me that I would not die, that he would
    make me immortal in a paradise of well-being.
But you, Iblis, are no longer the one whom I sought and
    found propitious, who could lead me by the halter,
and I shall give you just reward for the bad times into
    which you drove me, covering you with bloody
        wounds.

Farazdaq

*Iblis, possibly from Greek *diabolos,* the Arabic name of the Devil.

She rose to meet me with a kiss and embraced me
her limbs full, her mouth fragrant like musk.
"Come in, no one will know,
I am your ransom against suffering."
And so we lay that night, sleepless on our beds,
in the heat of passion she clasped me and I clasped her
until the two threads* appeared and I said to her,
"It is time to part," and grief almost overcame her.
Then I left her and no one knew of us.
May God reward her for her good deed.

Al-Walid II

*An allusion to Qur'an II, 183 concerning the fast of Ramadan:
"Eat and drink until a white thread can be distinguished from a black
thread in the dawn, and fast completely until nightfall."

She unclenched her fist and said, her tears flowing,
"Go away. You are not as they said. You are, by God,
   amorous and impudent.
Today my nurse is away and God alone can save me
   from you.
God, help me, see my weakness against this self-assured
   evildoer.
He grabbed at my bracelet and crushed it. He is strong,
   overpowering.
He pushed his beard against me, rough and black, like
   needles.
He came upon me when my kinsfolk were absent
but he would overbear them even were they present.
I swear by God, you shall not escape from them.
Then go away, for you are the triumphant attacker.
What will mother say when she sees my lips, what
   when you spread the news?
I have long feared the testing you brought on me,
what shall I say now?"

Bashshar ibn Burd

I love you with two loves,
one of passion, one that is your due.
In the love of passion, I constantly call on your name
    and no other.
In the love that is your due, you unveil and let me see you.
No praise to me for either of these loves;
praise to you alone for both of them.

Rabi'a al-'Adawiyya

Lord, though my sins are great and many
I know your forgiveness is greater still.
If only the virtuous can hope in you
from whom can the sinner seek refuge and help?
I call on you, Lord, humbly as you have commanded.
If you reject my hand, who will have pity?
I have no way to you but the hope
that you are forgiving, that I am a Muslim.

Abu Nuwas

By four things do heart and soul and body live:
Stream and garden, wine and happy face.

Abu Nuwas

I asked her for a kiss and obtained it
after refusal, and much effort.
By God, I said, my tormentress, be generous,
give me another and content me.
She smiled and cited a proverb,
known to the Persians, and true:
Never give anything to a child
who petulantly asks for another.

Abu Nuwas

I saw a palace beauty and fell in love with her
like the love of ʿUrwa the ʿUdhri* and the lover of
   Nahd†
When she persisted in coldness I said to her,
grant me your love, and she replied:
With such a face do you expect love from me?
If they sold faces in the market, I replied,
for ready cash and on any other terms,
I would change my face and buy another
hoping that then you might desire my wooing
for, though I am ugly, I am a poet.
Not even if you were Nabigha al-Jaʿdi,‡ she replied.

Abu Nuwas

---

*The Banu ʿUdhra were an Arabian tribe, famous for their devotion to poetry and their dedication to selfless, undemanding love, somewhat between platonic love and *l'amour courtois*. ʿUrwa ibn Hizam was the legendary model of ʿUdhri lovers.

†A reference to Ibn ʿAjlan al-Nahdi, a semi-legendary poet of the tribe of Nahd.

‡A poet who was a companion of the Prophet.

She whom I love sent me a messenger boy
and whoever is linked with her is also worthy of love.
Welcome messenger, I said, welcome friend
adorned with perfume.
I addressed caressing words to him and he drew back
saying, you want to tempt me.
Such a one as you cannot love such a one as I
when a flowering beauty is mad for him.
Then came other messengers with orders to go to her
and I went to her with a timid heart.
You fell in love with my messenger, she said.
Both this one and that one, you faithless lover,
will be recorded against you in the book of reckoning.
Whoever relies on the wolf in dealing with a kid
well deserves that the wolf should betray him.
And I replied, gentle and courteous,
with the same words that Jacob once spoke.
Indeed, one cannot trust the wolf,
but what they said about him and Joseph was a lie
when they threw Joseph into the well and said
it was the wolf who betrayed him.

Abu Nuwas

Nabat appeared before me all painted,
with her hair parted and washed in willow water.
She said, "I dyed myself with henna." I replied,
"No, it is not with henna that your fingertips are dyed,
No, those fingers are skilled in coquetry and wantonness
    as I tell you.
And why are your eyes anointed with kohl?"
"I used the kohl as salve," she said, "for a pain in my
    eye."
"Pardon me," I asked, "and why is your hair wet?"
"I was caught in the rain," she said, "and you were not."
"And why," I asked, "does your glistening garment flow
    loose?"
"I was constrained by this garment," she said,
    "oppressed by its weight."
She said, "Why all these questions, importunate one?"
I said, "I delight in what I see" and tears flowed from
    my eyes.
"You are overbearing," she said.
"This," I replied, "is your wantonness. What are these
    vain lies?"

Abu Nuwas

Friends, in the name of God,
dig my grave nowhere but Qutrabbul
amid the wine presses, in the vineyards.
Keep me far from the cornfields.
Perhaps in my ditch, I may hear
the stamping of feet in the wine presses.

Abu Nuwas

Pour me a drink, and another,
of the wine of Isfahan
or the wine of old Chosroes
or the wine of Qayrawan.
There is musk in the wine cup
or in the hand of the one who pours it;
or perhaps it was left in the wine
when they drew it from the jar.
Deck me with crown and diadem,
and sing me my own poems.
The wine cup is a springtime
you can touch with your fingers,
and the heat of the wine seeps slowly
from my tongue all the way to my feet.

Abu Nuwas

Your life is a sum of counted breaths.
With each breath that passes
a part of life is lost.
That which gives life brings death every moment
    nearer,
and your caravan is led by one
who will not jest with you.

Abuʾl-ʿAtahiya

I passed the whole night not closing my eyes.
The fleas like scattered fluff,
sated and half-sated bloodsuckers,
biting through hollow hairs,
plaguing the spirit if not destroying it,
boring into the skin, even through the cloak,
until it looked like the pointing* of the Holy Book
or like a spattering of prepared safflower.

Ibn al-Mu'tazz

*The Qur'anic text is usually fully vocalized, and thus includes numerous dots and dashes above and below the letters.

On a night that was like her hair, she poured for me
   that which was like her cheeks, and there was no
      censor.
Thus I lay two nights, of hair and of darkness,
   and two dawns, of wine and the beloved's face.

Ibn al-Muᶜtazz

.

A cloud, heavy with water,
came swaying astride the winds,
streamed through the night,
gushed and surged like blood from a wound.
The sky, revealed at dawn amid its stars,
seemed like a meadow of violets, moist with dew
and burgeoning camomile flowers.

Ibn al-Mu͑tazz

Only meet your lover by night
for the sun is a gossip and the night is a bawd.
Many a lover, when the darkness of night covers him,
meets his beloved while the slanderers sleep.

*Ibn al-Mu*ᶜ*tazz*

Your spirit is mingled with mine
as wine is mixed with water;
whatever touches you touches me.
In all the stations of the soul you are I.

Al-Hallaj

I am the One whom I love, and the One whom I love is
  myself.
We are two souls incarnated in one body;
if you see me, you see Him,
if you see Him, you see us.

Al-Hallaj

You glide between the heart and its casing as tears
    glide from the eyelid.
You dwell in my inwardness, in the depths of my heart,
    as souls dwell in bodies.
Nothing passes from rest to motion unless you move it
    in hidden ways.
O new moon.

Al-Hallaj

I am the noble and generous chief;
Your barking dogs annoy me.
Will they make the well-bred ill-bred?
Will they make the highborn lowborn?
They do not know me. If I live a little longer
the lance-points will show them my lineage.

Al-Mutanabbi

Tastier than old wine,
sweeter than the passing of winecups
is the play of swords and lances,
the clash of armies at my command.
To face death in battle is my life,
for life is what fulfils the soul.

Al-Mutanabbi

A heart that wine cannot console,
a life like the gifts of misers,
an age whose men are small
though their carcasses are gross.
I am not one of them though I live among them.
Gold ore in the dust and sand,
hares and yet they are kings,
open-eyed and asleep.
Death threatens their bodies
but their only enemy is food.
Their horses do not fall under a pierced rider in battle
but they stumble as if speared by a twig.
Your only friend is yourself, not he whom you call
    friend
though he multiply attention and flattery.
If respect could be won without wisdom,
the sword would never strike the swordsmith.
Like is drawn to like and the vilest
are the nearest of us to our vile world.
If none but the deserving could rise high,
the army would fly up and dust remain below.
If none should rule but those who merit it,
kings would be subjects and subjects kings.
Whoever has known women knows this—
they are lustrous outside and dark within.
If youth is tipsiness and age is care,
then life is death.

Al-Mutanabbi

My people made fate their henchman
    and strode across the peaks of epochs.
They swathed their heads with the sun
    and built their houses with the stars.
My forebear was Chosroes, of the towering palace—
    who among men has a forebear like mine?
The ancient power of royalty is mine,
    even above the honor of Islam and of culture.
I drew glory from the best of forebears
    and religion from the best of Prophets.
I based my pride on both sides,
    the majesty of the Persians and the religion of the Arabs.

Mihyar al-Daylami

How sad that man, after wandering freely through the
    world,
    is told by fate, "Go into the grave."
How many times have our feet in the dust of the earth
    trodden on a proud brow or a smiling face?

Abuʾl-ʿAlaʾ al Maʿarri

When we met to say farewell at morning
    the pennants fluttered in the palace court,
the proud horses gathered, the drums rolled,
    and the signals were set for parting.
We wept blood—as if our eyes
    were wounds from which the red tears flowed.
We had hoped to come again after three days,
    but how many more have been added to them!

Ibn Zaydun

How many nights we passed drinking wine
    until the marks of dawn appeared on the night.
The stars of dawn came to strike the darkness,
    and the stars of night fled, for night was conquered.
When we attained the best of all delights
    no care weighed on us, and no sorrow irked us.
Had this but remained, my joy would have endured,
    but the nights of union fell short.

Ibn Zaydun

My beauty drinks and gives me drink,
no spy disturbs us and no censor;
better so.

We lay a night of joy, of kisses and embraces—
"Where are you going, what do you want, why so
    restless?
Lavish your love on one who loves you—
whoever endures my passion will see my tenderness."
There is not much that I want
and do not get.

Youth is like what it does
then let it come and dally.
I have seen many things, but none more beautiful
than this bosom that incites me to embrace it,
than the firm breasts that jut from it
provokingly.

A little mouth like a ring
with pearls that no jeweller strung,
temptation for him who prays and him who fasts.
My exposition is not accurate—
I said her mouth is like a ring
but it is better.

The talk goes on, the wine is drunk,
I sing and she makes music.
I ask of her—what one asks;
she says "yes," and grants my wishes.
Dawn is rising, the oppressor,
why does it rise?

I got up to take my cloak, not delaying.
She said, "Where are you going, what do you want to
    do?
Take off your cloak, stay with me a while."
I said, "I am going in search of gold, let me be,
I am going to Abu'l-Qasim ibn Sumayda͑,
I want to praise him.

He from whose wealth so much is hoped.
Of his bounty and his benefaction
all his retainers speak.
Look at his splendor and tell me,
Hatim[*] has become a proverb for generosity
he is more generous."

Ibn Quzman

[*]A legendary figure of ancient Arabia, cited as the model of open-
handed generosity.

While the sun's eye rules my sight,
love sits as sultan in my soul.
His army has made camp in my heart—
passion and yearning, affliction and grief.
When his camp took possession of me
I cried out as the flame of desire
burned in my entrails.
Love stole my sleep, love has bewildered me,
love kills me unjustly, and I am helpless;
love has burdened me with more than I can bear
so that I bequeath him a soul and no body.

Ibn al-ʿArabi

Enrich me with the flood of love that wells within you
and take pity on this tinder in the fire your passion has
   kindled
and if I ask to see you in reality,
grant it, and do not answer: "Thou shalt not see!"*
O my heart, you promised me patience in this love,
therefore endure, though you be anguished and
   tormented.
For love is life, and if you perish in its rapture
your reward is to die and be forgiven.

ᶜUmar ibn al-Farid

*God's answer to a similar request from Moses, as given in the
Qurʾan VII, 143.

Spring has come with his whites and his blacks—
    two classes, his lords and his slaves;
the branches are his army of spears, and above
    the leaves are his unfurled flags.

Ibn Sahl al-Andalusi

The Faith of a Lover

My grief? It leaves a burning coal in my heart.
　You see it on his cheek, moistened and cooled.
He asks me: "Of what faith?" "A mocker!"
　for all my belief is squandered in love of him.
My heart is my true believer, but my eye
　is a Magian, adoring the fire of his cheek.

Ibn Sahl al-Andalusi

I used to shun my companion
if his religion was not like mine;
but now my heart accepts every form.
It is a pasturage for gazelles, a monastery for monks,
a temple of idols, a Ka'ba for the pilgrim,
the tables of the Torah, the holy book of the Qur'an.
Love alone is my religion, and whichever way
its horses turn, that is my faith and creed.

Anonymous

A literary circle in a ruler's palace, probably gathered to
educate a young prince.

A literary picnic.

Joseph in the pit, accompanied by the archangel Gabriel.

The Sasanid Shah Bahram Ghur on his throne, having
killed two lions.

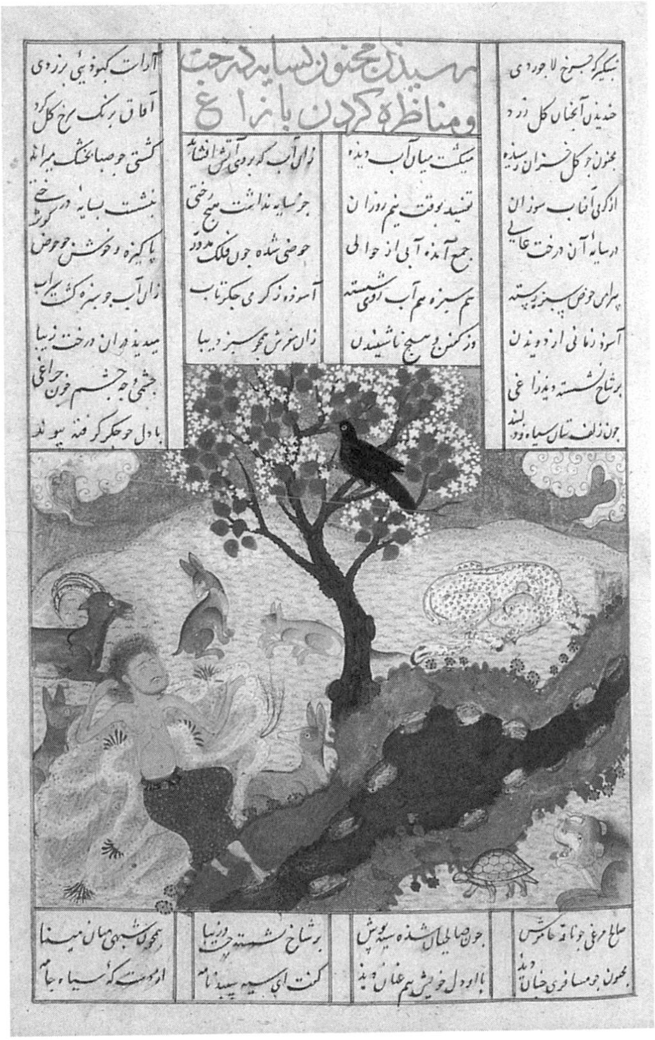

Majnun seeking refuge in the wilderness.

The Sasanid Shah Khusraw, with the architect Farhad.

King Solomon holding court, with angels and animals as well as humans in attendance.

Persian Shah hunting with cheetah and falcon.

Persian Poems

She said to me: This is God's paradise, not a garden.
I said: This is a garden, blissful as God's paradise
but that one is unseen, this one is seen,
that is credit, this is cash,
that is hidden, this revealed,
that earned by prayer, this by eulogy,
that is God's grace, this the king's bounty.

Rudagi

Kisses are like salt water,
The more you drink, the more you thirst.

Rudagi

Live in joy with joyous black-eyed girls,
for life is just a tale, a breath.
Be open to the present,
silent on the past.
All I want is scented tresses,
the houri-sprung moon-faced one.
Happy he who gave and could take pleasure,
unhappy he who neither took nor gave.
This world is wind and cloud and mirage.
Pour more wine, for what will be, will be.

Rudagi

Though my heart bleeds with pain of parting
pain I endure for you is more joy than pain
each night I ponder, and I say "O God,
if such is parting from her, how will union be?"

Rudagi

This is wine—if the merest driblet falls in the Nile,
its scent makes the sober crocodile drunk without end.
If the deer on the plain drinks but a single drop,
he becomes a roaring lion, fearing no tiger.

Rudagi

When you see me dead, my lips forever closed
and see this passion-racked form empty of life,
you can sit by my bedside and say, so charmingly,
it was I who killed you, and now I am sorry.

Rudagi

Wine Song

Wine shows man's mettle,
marks freeborn from slave,
noble from base.
How much art in this potion!
When you drink, there is joy
while rose and jasmine bloom.

How many a high tower wine has breached,
how many a wild colt wine has tamed,
how many a miser, drinking wine,
showers his bounty on the world.

Rudagi

All the teeth I ever had are rotted or gone
once they were not teeth but glowing lamps,
silver white, pearls and corals,
morning stars and drops of rain.
Not one remains now, all decayed and fallen out—
by what ill-omened star? Was it baleful Saturn? . . .

You moon-faced girl with musky tresses
what can you know of how I used to be?
You flaunt your curls in front of me,
you did not see me when I too had curls.
Gone is the time when my face was like satin,
my hair like jet. . . .

I used to buy—and weighed out countless dirhams—
whenever there was a Turkish girl in town, with
     pomegranate breasts.
How many pretty girls took a fancy to me
and came to see me furtively by night,
not daring to come by day
for fear of their master or of jail.
Glowing wine, a pretty boy, a girl's face—
they may have been costly, but they were cheap for me.
My heart was a full treasury, a treasure of words. . . .

O moon-faced girl, you see Rudagi now,
you never saw me as I used to be. . . .
Time has changed and I have changed. Bring me my
     stick
for now it is the time for staff and scrip.

Rudagi

I do not dye my hair black
so as to be young again and sin again
but because people dye their clothes black in
   mourning,
so I have dyed my hair black, mourning my old age.

Rudagi

O my idol, a cloud from heaven has dressed the world
in the bright garb of April.
The rose-bower is like Eden,
the flowering tree like a houri of Paradise
the earth a bloodstained brocade
the sky a kerchief dyed with indigo.
The world is so changed, you would think
the leopard pounces on the doe only in play . . .

an idol with ruby cheek, red wine gleaming
like the vestments in the temple.
The world preens like a peacock,
sometimes tender, sometimes fierce.
You would see, in the wine and the musk
the likeness of the Beloved traced on the meadow.
From the soil rises such a scent of rose water
you would think there were roses crushed into the soil.
Daqiqi has chosen four things
from all the good and evil in the world—
ruby lips, the flute's lament,
limpid wine, and the faith of Zoroaster.

Daqiqi

They said be patient, patience will bear fruit.
I suppose it will, but in another life.
I have spent my whole life being patient.
I'll need another life to reap the fruits.

Daqiqi

Kingship

There are two things with which men gain a kingdom,
one steel blue and one of saffron color.
One is gold, stamped with the king's name,
the other iron, tempered in the Yemen.
Whoever aspires to kingship
must have an urge from heaven,
an eloquent tongue, a liberal hand,
a heart both vengeful and loving.
For kingship is a quarry that cannot be caught
by a soaring eagle or raging lion.
Only two things can make it captive—
a well-forged blade, and mined and minted gold.
Seize it with the sword,
chain it, if you can, with gold coins.
Whoever has sword, money, and luck
needs neither lofty stature nor royal pedigree,
but only wisdom, munificence, and courage
for heaven to grant him the gift of sovereignty.

Daqiqi

With a caravan of cloths I left Sistan
with cloths spun from the heart, woven from the soul
cloths made of a silk which is called Word
cloths designed by an artist who is called Tongue
every stitch was drawn by force from the breast
every weft separated in torment from the heart.
These are not woven cloths like any cloth
do not judge them in the same way as others . . .
This is no cloth that can be spoilt by water
this is no cloth that can be damaged by fire
its color is not destroyed by the earth's dust
nor its design effaced by the passing of time.

Farrukhi

If coming had been my choice, I would not have come.
If going were my choice, would I ever go?
Better this ruined abode had never seen me,
not come, not stay, not go.

Sana'i

In one hand the Qur'an, in the other a wineglass,
sometimes keeping the rules, sometimes breaking
  them.
Here we are in this world, unripe and raw,
not outright heathens, not quite Muslims.

Mujir

Heart, reckon you have gained all the treasures of this
    world
reckon the garden of your joy is adorned with green
on this green grass reckon you are the dew
falling by night and vanishing at dawn.

I am not one to tremble faced with death
creation's other half is more welcome to me than this
I have a soul God lent me
I shall return it when it falls due.

Whoever in this world has half a loaf
enough for shelter and for sustenance
who is no man's servant and no man's master
let him be happy, for mortal bliss is his.

ʿOmar Khayyam

From evening till morning the fleas were dancing
   to the fluting of the gnats
around on my body—and I joined with them merrily,
   scratching the harp.

Anvari

If you pass by Samarqand O light morning breeze[*]
carry a letter to the court of the prince from the people
   of Khurasan
a letter that begins with pain of body and grief of soul
a letter that ends with heartbreak and agony
a letter whose lines reveal the sighs of strangers
a letter whose folds hide the blood of martyrs
its texts dried by the sighs of the oppressed
its heading moist from the weeping of the bereaved
reading it, the throat grows sore
seeing it, the eye is suffused with blood . . .

Deign to hear the story of the sad people of Khurasan
and, having heard it, deign to look at them.
They ask, from wounded hearts and tortured entrails
O victorious protector of hearts, of the faith, of the
   realm,
has word reached you that by the rack and ruin of the
   Ghuzz
not a span of land in Khurasan remains unruined?
Has word reached you that of all that was good
today no trace remains in all Iran?
Those who were princes are now underlings of
   chieftains
vile grooms now command the noble

---

[*]This poem, addressed by the poet to the ruler of Samarqand, in-
forms him of the plight of Khurasan, invaded by the Ghuzz tribes,
and asks for help.

the well-born knock, sad and confused, on the doors of
 the base-born
the virtuous are tormented captives in the hands of
 libertines
you see no man happy save on his deathbed
no girl a virgin save at her mother's breast.
In every city the mosques are stalls for their beasts
made into stables without roof or door
no prayer is recited in the name of the Ghuzz
in Khurasan now there is no preacher, no pulpit . . .
Save the people from this affliction, O royal born,
free the realm from this torment, O pure of lineage.
By God who graced the dinar with your name
by God who placed the crown on your head
make God's people free and safe
from these worthless, ill-omened plundering Ghuzz . . .

O king, you are a splendid sun and Khurasan is ruins
but does not the sun shine on ruins as on prosperity?
Iran is like a salty desert and you are a cloud
but does not the cloud scatter rain over deserts as it
does over gardens? . . .

Anvari

Parted from you I said I feared for my life.
Now joined to you I am still afraid.
Yesterday I feared the tongues of my enemies.
Today I fear the eyes of my friends.

Jamaluddin Mohammad Isfahani

In the garden of my life sorrow is gardener,
no tree or bush is left, no rose, no tulip.
On the threshing-floor of time, from so much pain
no ear or grain is left, no straw, no dust.

This life and all existence are nothing,
this ancient home and bed are also nothing.
For the credit and the cash by which we live
youth is the capital, and youth too is nothing.

Khaqani

I am sunk, deep at the bottom of a sea of misery
bewildered, like a pearl oyster, without hand or foot.
Heaven, to seize that royal pearl,
shatters the oyster shell of my heart.

Khaqani

They say that from the womb of nothingness
    once in a thousand years a noble man is born
he lived before I came into this world
    he will return when, grieving, I am gone.

Two remote poles plunge my heart into mourning
    set fire to my breast and torture my mind
they are—if you are not afraid to hear my confession—
    my vanished youth and my departed friends.

Don't sleep, your color is like pomegranate flowers
    don't sleep, honey and rubies meet in your lips
don't sleep, O languorous and deadly narcissus
    this is a night of festival. Don't sleep.

Khaqani

The spring of youth has gone its dismal way,
    it gave me only pain the livelong day.
My life is blank like death and all my song
    is but a dirge for lights that melt away.

Khaqani

Reckon my friend, the sum of life
from this two-colored screed of evenings and of dawns.
Besides the falsified script of night and day
what have you gained from this abode of sorrow?
The world is a banquet of poisoned food,
life is a dream interpreted by death.

Khaqani

Though my master speaks ill of me
I shall not mar my face with pain.
I shall speak nothing but good of him
so that we may both be seen as liars.

Kamaluddin Isma'il Isfahani

First, the king asked him, "Where are you from?"
He replied: "From the capital of the realm of love."

"And what trade do they follow there?"
"They buy grief and sell souls."

"But selling souls is not good work."
"But not unknown to lovers."

"Did you fall in love with all your heart?"
"You speak of heart. I speak of soul."

"Do you see her every night like the lustrous moon?"
"Yes, when sleep comes—but where is my sleep?"

"When will you free your heart from love of her?"
"When at last I sleep beneath the earth."

"And if you could stride into her palace?"
"I would throw my head beneath her feet."

"And if she were to wound your eye?"
"I would offer her the other eye."

"And if another were to clasp her?"
"He would taste my steel though he be hard as stone."

"And if you never find a way to reach her?"
"One may gaze on the moon from afar . . ."

"And if she asked you for all that you possess?"
"For that I pray weeping to God."

"And if only your head would satisfy her?"
"I would strike this borrowed head from my body . . ."

"Rid your heart and mind of this love."
"This should never be asked of a lover."

"Calm down, for what you seek is vain and foolish."
"Calm is something that is forbidden to me."

"Then go, and patiently endure your pain."
"How can there be patience without soul or life?"

"But patience of the heart is no shame."
"The heart may be patient but I have no more heart."

"In your pain do you then fear no one?"
"I fear only the torment of separation from her . . ."*

Nizami

*This dialogue is an extract from a long narrative poem entitled "Khusraw and Shirin" about the Persian Shah Khusraw and the Armenian Christian Princess Shirin. The stonemason (or architect) Farhad meets the Princess and falls hopelessly in love with her. The Shah, hearing of this, summons and interrogates him and finding that he cannot discourage Farhad's love, deals with him in another way. He sends him a false report of Shirin's death, whereupon Farhad throws himself from a mountaintop to his death. The Shah meets Shirin again, and after some discussion they are reconciled and marry.

I shall grasp the soul's skirt with my hand
and stamp on the world's head with my foot.
I shall trample Matter and Space with my horse,
beyond all Being I shall utter a great shout,
and in that moment when I shall be alone with Him,
I shall whisper secrets to all mankind.
Since I shall have neither sign nor name
I shall speak only of things unnamed and without sign.
Do not delude yourself that from a burned heart
I will discourse with palate and tongue.
The body is impure, I shall cast it away
and utter these pure words with soul alone.

Attar

In a Baghdad street a Sufi passed one day
and heard a pedlar cry
"Here is honey, plenty of honey,
going cheap, who will buy?"
Said the Sufi: "O patient pedlar
would you give some for nothing?"—"God forbid!
Are you mad, my friend? What bug has bitten you?
Who ever gives anything for nothing?"
But a voice spoke from on high: "Come, Sufi,
try a little harder, rise a step higher,
and you will receive all from me for nothing
and if you wish it, even more."

ᶜ*Attar*

If the image of our Beloved is in the heathen temple
then it is flagrant error to walk round the Kaʿba*
if in the Kaʿba His fragrance is not present
then it is but a synagogue
and if in the synagogue we sense the fragrance of union
    with Him
then that synagogue is our Kaʿba

Jalaluddin Rumi

*The Kaʿba is the sanctuary in Mecca, the holiest of holy places
for Muslims.

What can I do, Muslims? I do not know myself.
I am neither Christian nor Jew, neither Magian nor
  Muslim,
I am not from east or west, not from land or sea,
not from the shafts of nature nor from the spheres of
  the firmament,
not of the earth, not of water, not of air, not of fire.
I am not from the highest heaven, not from this world,
not from existence, not from being.
I am not from India, not from China, not from Bulgar,
  not from Saqsin,
not from the realm of the two Iraqs, not from the land
  of Khurasan.
I am not from the world, not from the beyond,
not from heaven and not from hell.
I am not from Adam, not from Eve, not from paradise
  and not from Ridwan.
My place is placeless, my trace is traceless,
no body, no soul, I am from the soul of souls.
I have chased out duality, lived the two worlds as one.
One I seek, one I know, one I see, one I call.
He is the first, he is the last, he is the outer, he is the
  inner.
Beyond "He" and "He is" I know no other.
I am drunk from the cup of love, the two worlds have
  escaped me.
I have no concern but carouse and rapture.
If one day in my life I spend a moment without you
from that hour and that time I would repent my life.
If one day I am given a moment in solitude with you

I will trample the two worlds underfoot and dance
     forever.
O Sun of Tabriz, I am so tipsy here in this world,
I have no tale to tell but tipsiness and rapture.

Jalaluddin Rumi

The man of God is drunk without wine
the man of God is sated without meat

the man of God is distraught and amazed
the man of God does not eat or sleep

the man of God is a king under the cowl
the man of God is a treasure in a ruined place

the man of God is not of air and earth
the man of God is not of fire and water

the man of God is a sea without shores
the man of God rains pearls without a cloud

the man of God has a hundred moons and skies
the man of God has a hundred suns

the man of God is made wise by truth
the man of God is not learned from books

the man of God is beyond belief and unbelief
the man of God is beyond evil and good

the man of God comes riding from nothingness
the man of God rides nobly accoutred

the man of God is hidden, sun of the faith,
the man of God, seek and you will find him.

Jalaluddin Rumi

The Moth and the Candle

I remember one sleepless night
I heard the moth say to the candle
"I am in love, it is proper that I burn,
but why are you tormented and aflame?"
"O my poor lover," the candle made reply,
"my sweet love the honey is parted from me
and since his sweetness has gone,
like Farhad, a fire consumes me."
At every moment, as the candle spoke, a flood of grief
flowed down her pallid cheek.
"Presumptuous one! Love is not for you.
With neither patience nor the power to endure
you flee at the slightest touch of flame
while I stand firm till I am utterly consumed;
you flee if the flame of love singes your wing tip
while I burn from head to foot.
Don't look at my brilliance that illuminates all around,
look at my burning fever, my heart-rending flow of
      tears."
Only part of the night had passed in this way
When suddenly a fairy-faced beauty quenched the
      candle
and said, as the smoke was rising,
"This is the end of love, young man,
this is the way, if you want to learn.
Only quenching can save you from the fire."

                                        Sa'di

He who built the heavens and made the stars
and fashioned mind and soul and made mankind
tied all the strings of being in a knot
then lost the thread of this cosmic tangle.

ʿUbayd-i Zakani

Lord, of your grace all that I hope is this—
keep the realm of my pleasure prosperous
avert from me the calamity of chastity
and keep far from me the doom of repentence.

ʿUbayd-i Zakani

I used to have a little farm
    which gave me what I needed every year.
In my house there was always some plain bread, some
      greens,
    for any guest who chanced to call
and sometimes even a cup of wine prepared
    for a drinking friend or a pretty girl,
But now I have neither bread nor wine,
    of what I owned nothing is left.
In my house only I myself remain
    and I would not stay were I good for anything.

                      ʿUbayd-i Zakani

Do not delve deeply as I have done in the sciences
lest princes despise you as they do me.
Do you wish to be accepted by the rulers of the world?
Play the libertine, the singer, the shameless beggar.

ʿUbayd-i Zakani

Hair disheveled, smiling lips, sweating and tipsy,
garment torn, singing a love song, glass in hand,
picking a quarrel, chanting a spell,
yesterday at midnight she came and sat by my bed.

She lowered her head to my ear, and whispered,
    sad-voiced,
"My old lover, are you asleep?"
The lover for whom such a nightfarer's drink is poured
is an unbeliever of love if he does not worship wine.

Come on, hermit, do not blame those who drink to the
    dregs,
there was no other gift when God announced His
    Mastery.
The smile of the wineglass, a girl's tangled tresses,
have broken many penances, as they broke the penance
    of Hafiz.

Hafiz

Cupbearer, it is morning, fill my cup with wine.
Make haste, the heavenly sphere knows no delay.
Before this transient world is ruined and destroyed,
ruin me with a beaker of rose-tinted wine.
The sun of the wine dawns in the east of the goblet.
Pursue life's pleasure, abandon dreams,
and the day when the wheel makes pitchers of my clay,
take care to fill my skull with wine!
We are not men for piety, penance and preaching
but rather give us a sermon in praise of a cup of clear
    wine.
Wine-worship is a noble task, O Hafiz;
rise and advance firmly to your noble task.

Hafiz

The rose came like a bride
to a feast in the rose bower.
Where is the eloquent nightingale? Let it sing its song!
Heart! Don't mourn because of parting; the world
holds both grief and joy, thorn and rose, pit and peak.
I am bent like a bow with sorrow, but I do not say
    goodbye
to thoughts of brows like bows and eyes that shoot
    arrows.
Because of your kiss-curl, my heart is bewildered;
no wonder if the musk-scented one is a gossip.
With tipsy heart I lay my face
upon your threshold, not just now, but for an eternity of
    fire and pain.
Rough and smooth are the same in Hafiz's way.
What matter peak and valley for a bird?

Hafiz

Last night I saw angels knock at the tavern door.
They kneaded Adam's clay into wine cups.
The dwellers of the secret sanctuary, the pure of
  angelhood,
were vagrants with me, drinking the wine of the
  drunken.
All heaven could not hold the entrusted pledge.
The lot was drawn, and madness fell to me.
The strife of seventy-two sects may be forgiven,
they could not see the truth and strayed to illusion.
Thanks be to God, there is peace between Him and me,
the dancing Sufis empty the cup of gratitude.
It is not the fire that makes the candle smile
but it is the fire that burns the moth.
None more than Hafiz has unveiled the cheek of
  thought
Since men first combed the locks of words with pens.

Hafiz

If life remains, I shall go back to the tavern
and do no other work than serve the revellers.
Happy day when, with streaming eyes,
I shall go again to sprinkle the tavern floor.
There is no knowledge among these folk,
Suffer me, God, to offer my jewel of self to another
    buyer.
If the Friend has gone, rejecting the claim of old
    friendship,
God forbid I should go and look for another friend.
If the turn of the heavenly wheel favor me
I shall find some other craft to bring him back.

My soul seeks wholeness, if that be permitted
by his wanton glance and bandit tresses.
See our guarded secret, a ballad sung
with drum and flute at the gate of another bazaar.
Every moment I sigh in sorrow, for fate, every hour
strikes at my wounded heart with another torment.
Yet truly I say: Hafiz is not alone in this plight;
So many others were swallowed in this desert.

Hafiz

A group of dervishes.

Layla and Qays at school.

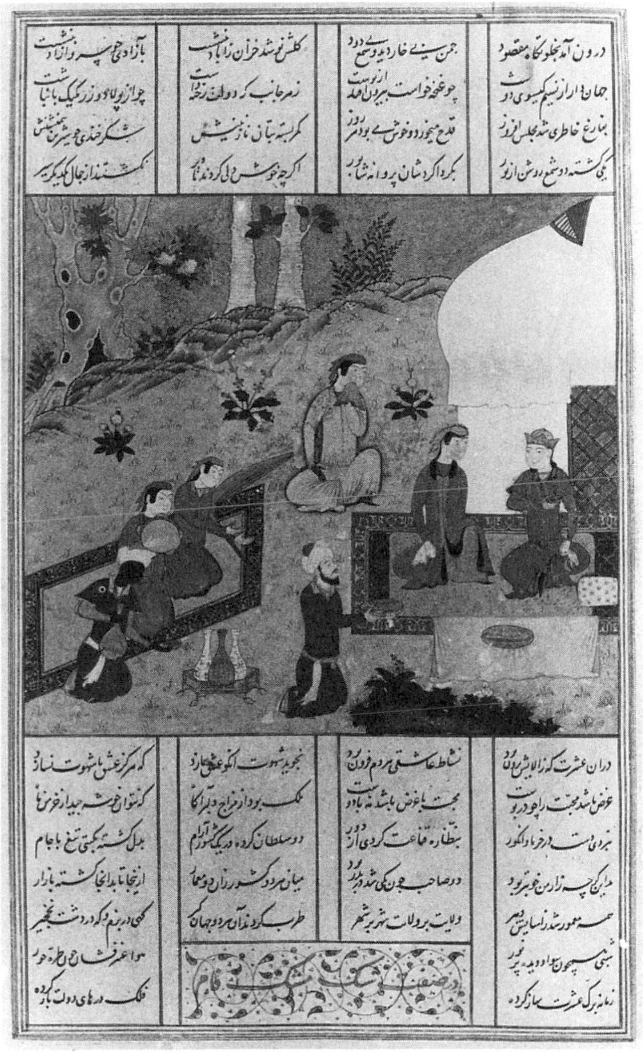

Khusraw and Shirin.

Jalaluddin Rumi meets his disciple Molla Shams al-Din.

Sheykh Bahauddin Valad preaching in Balkh.

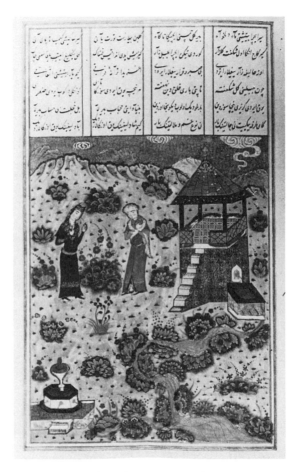

Layla and Majnun together.

Lovers.

Evening entertainment and festival in the harem. Two
miniatures pasted on the same folio. The lower picture shows
an evening festival, for men only. Masked players dance. The
upper picture depicts a couple with attendants, while
musicians and dancers prepare to perform.

Woman looking at a mirror.

Young woman with a rose,
by Levni.

A dancing girl, by Levni.

Turkish
Poems

To be slave to a king who can never be dethroned,
to lean on a threshold whence none can be wrested,

to be a bird and fly to a far place,
to drink of a wine from which there is no sobering,

to be a strong swimmer and plunge into the sea,
to bring out a jewel that no jeweler knows,

to enter a garden and take pleasure,
to sniff a rose that never fades,

Man must be Lover, find his Beloved,
burn in the fire of love and in no other.

Yunus, desist from thought of existence, turn your face
    in worship.
Bring a man like your true self, whose like the world
    can never know.

Yunus Emre

Let the deaf listen to the dumb,
let the soul understand them both.
We understood before we heard
acted before we understood.

On this path, for a man of truth,
his capital is nothingness.
We loved and were loved,
became Lover and Beloved.
Every instant born anew,
who can grow weary of you?

He spoke in seventy-two tongues,
a word fell between them.
So we saw all together,
not blaming great or small.

Yunus, if you wish, be holy.
Earth and heaven brim with holiness.
A thousand Moses are hidden under every stone.

Yunus Emre

My picture, my darling, my friend, my boon
    companion, my intimate, my soul,
my comrade, my confidant, my life, my spirit, my
    remedy for grief,
my sovereign, my moon, my sweetheart, my being, my
    sustenance, my spirit,
my refuge, my goal, my direction, my orbit, my
    thought, my soul,
my moon-featured, fairy-faced one, my merry and
    wanton charmer,
my jasmine-scented, rose fragrant one, my cypress
    grown in a rose garden,
my delicate, my elegant one, my fair, my dear one, my
    peerless beloved,
my Hijaz,* my Ka'ba, my Sinai, my paradise, my houri,
    my Ridvan,†
my rose, my sweet basil, my trees, my ambergris, my
    aloe wood,
my pearl, my precious metal, my ruby, my carnelian,
    my coral,
my heart illuminating, faithful, entrail-kindling
    tormentor,
my sovereign, my world conqueror, my ruler, my
    monarch and emperor,
my candle, my lamp, my light, my radiance, my star,
    my sun,
my nightingale, my bulbul, my rose, I am sweet-toned
    Nesimi.

Nesimi

---

*The region in Arabia in which the holy cities of Mecca and Me-
dina are situated.   †The angel who guards the gate of Paradise.

My purpose is to obey God's command to wage jihad,
my zeal is for the faith of Islam alone.
By the grace of God and the brave men of God's army,
my purpose is to conquer the infidels entirely.
My trust is in the Prophets and the saints,
my hope of victory and conquest is in God's bounty.
What if I wage jihad with life and fortune?
Praise be to God, my desire for battle grows many
    thousandfold.
O Muhammad, by your own miracles
let my power triumph over the enemies of the faith.

Sultan Mehmed II

Woman, they say, is deficient in sense
so they ought to pardon her every word.
But one female who knows what to do
is better than a thousand males who don't.

Mihri Hatun

I opened my eyes from sleep and suddenly raised my
head;
before me I saw standing a moon-faced, heart-rending
beauty.
My star was lucky or, perhaps, I attained the Night of
Power.
I saw the planet Jupiter rise in my street that night,
I saw light flowing from his beauty,
he looked like a Muslim but wore the clothes of an
unbeliever.
In the blink of an eye he vanished from sight,
but as I saw him he was either angel or sprite.
Mihri is immortal until the day of resurrection, because
she has attained the elixir of life,
because in the darkness of night she saw Iskender plain.

Mihri Hatun

Heedless friend, ruthless fate, restless time,
endless pain with none to share, mighty foe and feeble
  star.
The shade of hope fades, the sun of desire burns,
the rank of adversity is lofty, the grade of precaution
  lowly,
wisdom falls short, censure resounds ever higher,
destiny has little compassion, love's misfortune grows
  day by day.
I am a stranger in the realm of passion, in paths of
  deceit and confusion,
I am a plain fellow in a world full of painting and magic.
The sight of every slender-waisted one is a flooding
  torrent of calamity,
the brow of every crescent-browed girl is the heading of
  a copybook of madness,
the dignity of learning is vagrant like a tulip petal in the
  wind,
the mark of fortune inverted, like a willow reflected in
  water.
The frontier of heart's desire is a toilsome testing road,
the relays of quest a pain-laden way of endeavor.
The witness of attainment is hidden like a harp note,
the cup of conviviality is upturned like limpid bubbles
  in wine.
Discord has arisen, the world goes a fearsome way.
I don't know, what shall I do, there is no willing guide.
Fuzuli's red tears have covered his sallow face.
See to what sickly hue the blue skies have reduced him.

Fuzuli

Let none be downcast and afflicted as I am, O God,
the thrall of the pangs of love and the wound of
parting, O God.
I suffer ceaseless pain from these merciless goddesses—
let no Muslim be slave to these infidels, O God.
I see that moon-faced one seeking my death; that is my
sorrow.
May she not need to suffer remorse, O God.
If they wish to draw her arrow from my flesh,
let them take the wounded heart but not the arrow, O
God.
I have grown used to pain, what would I be without it?
Let there be no limit to that pain, no end to that
torment, O God.
Do not say that in her is no justice, or much injustice,
for come what may,
on the throne of my heart let there be no sovereign but
she, O God.
In the corner of the tavern, Fuzuli found a treasure of
contentment,
a blessed realm. Let not that realm be ruined, O God.

Fuzuli

Gazel

My love has tired me of my life—will she not tire of
   cruelty?
My sigh has set the spheres on fire—will not the candle
   of my passion burn?

On those who faint and fail for her, my love bestows a
   healing balm.
Why does she give none to me; does she not think that
   I am sick?

I hid my pain from her. They said tell it to your love.
And if I tell that faithless one—I do not know, will she
   believe, or will she not?

In the night of separation, my soul burns, my eyes
   weep blood.
My cries awaken: does my black fate never wake?

Against the rose of your cheek, red tears stream from
   my eyes.
Dear love, this is the time of roses, will not these
   flowing waters cloud?

It was not I who turned to you but you who drove my
   sense away.
When the fool who blames me sees you, will he not be
   put to shame?

Fuzuli is a crazy lover and a byword among folk.
Ask then what kind of love is this—of such a love does
   he not tire?

                                        Fuzuli

My stock is Albanian,
all my race live by the sword.
What if this lion-quelling people,
like falcons, make their home in the rocks?
This is the merit of the Albanian—
He is like a jewel in the stone.

Yahya of Tashlija

What are these smiles, these wiles, this coquetry and
   this disdain?

What is this grace, these airs, this lofty stature?

What is this downy cheek, this eye, this brow,

this amber mole, this black beauty spot?

What are these curling, whirling, twisting, turning
   tresses,

these plaited locks, these coiled and musky curls?

Is your waist the thread of life, your breast a silver
   mirror?

Your ear and earring are like a dew-flecked rose.

Unhopeful of loyalty, undaunted by cruelty, Baki is in
   love.

For him the squandering of his heart is fitting, for you,
   disdain.

Baki

Cupbearer! The wineglass makes a beautiful rose—
he who takes it in his hand becomes a nightingale.

Whoever sees the fresh wound in my breast
will admire a beautiful red carnation.

The pale breath of my sigh of longing for your lovelock
becomes a slender blue hyacinth.

Whoever explores the locks of the beloved
becomes enmeshed and bound in her tresses.

If the waters of attainment do not save Baki,
he will burn to a cinder in the fire of separation.

Baki

Since there is no permanence in this world of ruin,
a thousand years, a single moment, count the same.

Rose time has come, the world is fresh and young again.
Feast and roister while you are young.

Sufi! Don't deny the goodness of wine—
The Master of wisdom ordained it so in a book . . .

There is no choice but to come, moaning, to your door.
By God, sir, in this respect I am not at fault.

Baki, seeing the cupbearer's cheek reflected in the
    winecup,
thinks it is the flaming sun at dawn.

Baki

Your cheek is like fresh water,
your chin like a bubble.

The sunbeams of your cheek strike my heart
like moonlight on the water.

By your skilled penmanship, the page of my heart
is like an illuminated book.

At the feast of sorrow my bloodshot eyes
are like two winecups.

Love for that moon grips the whole world
like the light of the sun.

O Baki, the perfumed mole of the beloved
is like pure musk, scented and black.

Baki

Greetings from me to the Bey of Bolu.*
Let him come and lean against these mountains,
let the mountains echo and reecho
the sound of the clash of arrows.
The enemy has come, in ranks;
the black script of fate is written on my white brow;
the musket has come, manhood is spoilt;
the curved sword must rust in its scabbard.
Has Köroğlu fallen from his glory?
He sends many from the battlefield.
Our boots are filled, our garments are stained
with the horse's spittle and the foeman's blood.

Köroğlu

---

*The governor of the district of Bolu, in northwest Turkey.

The Beys of our lands
light their candles,
they drink and become lions
and twirl their glasses round.
They drink till they are full
and then go out to seek a foe.
They mount their Arab horses,
stretching out their necks.
But my heart has rotted, rotted,
and my guts melt inside.
The arms of the Beys are weary
from brandishing the sword.
Beys, now what shall we do?
Let us go off with the girls,
let us show off our horses in the square,
stretching out their necks.
Köroğlu says: I have grown old,
I have aged and I have rotted.
My horse is tired and I am tired
of giving girls a ride.

Köroğlu

My tipsy darling, what magic made you so bold,
made you taller than a cypress?

Your tender flesh is more fragrant than perfume, more
limpid than color
as if a particolored rose had nourished you at its
breast—

You wear a rose-patterned brocade, and I fear for you,
my darling,
a scratch from the shade of the thorn of the rose on
that brocade—

You came with a rose in one hand, a cup in the other,
which should I take, the rose, the cup, or you?

Nedim

Nedim to His Heart

When the morning wind blows, you are cast down,
 my heart,
like a slave enmeshed in the beloved's tresses.
In the season of roses, it seems to me, my heart,
you too repent, as I, of forswearing wine.
Did I bid you drink no wine, love no beauty?
Then why do you shun me so, my heart?
You and my mind treat each other as strangers
as if you were a guest in my body, you, my heart.
Like a caravan lamp on the pilgrim's road
you are seen among the master craftsmen of love, my
 heart.
Since you have offered Nedim the cup of love
Be kind, don't take it back, let him rejoice awhile.

Nedim

We understand the purpose of that glance,
we have some sense.
We may lack words but we are not unaware—
Surely we won't refuse the cup she offers, the coquette,
that was our pact with her, our agreement.
"I have a humble house near Beshiktash,
just right for you, my sweet. Come, get the title deeds."
If any pious man has problems loving,
let him ask me, for in that art
I have done much research, acquired much skill.
Every night, others clasp your waist, join heart to heart.
Tyrant, be just, I too have a heart.
Don't fret, come to the feast.
There will be no strangers, and the only guests
I, Nedim, your slave, and you, my Sultan.

Nedim

If I say that the skies have opened, the spring has
   come,
I mean that my beloved has shown me some affection.

If I say that the meadow is adorned with blossoms,
it conveys that my sweetheart spoke to me with a smile.

Şeyh Galib

Were I your treasure, you would squander me,
were I your mirror, you would dazzle me.
From the arrow of the eye to the scar of the heart,
just look, and what sights you will see.
Cupbearer, inspiration is either with you or with me,
you are making the sea the guest of bubbles.
With passionate looks, O eye,
you have made fire and water the same.
O pious man, that moonlike beauty is such a light
you cannot call it an idol, you may believe.
Words are less than the sound of an empty drum.
Galib! You lament in vain.
Respond to the music of the spheres, be a Mevlevi,[*]
and you will meditate and you will turn.

Şeyh Galib

---

[*]A member of the dervish fraternity founded by Mevlana (or
Mawlana) Jalaluddin Rumi.

You are my Master. If I have some credit in the world,
    it comes from you.
If I have some fame among lovers, it comes from you.

You are the plenitude of my life, my soul and spirit:
if there is some gain on the capital of my life, it comes
    from you.

The color of your beauty gives reality to this imagined
    form;
if there is spring in the rose garden of my dream, it
    comes from you.

I have suffered no atom of pain at the hands of fate:
O bright sun, if I moan and weep, it comes from you.

You are the candle of union, I the moth of your flame:
if I yearn every night to kiss and embrace, it comes
    from you.

I have become a martyr of your love; my breast is a
    tulip bed of wounds;
if there is a lamp on my grave, a candle in my tomb, it
    comes from you.

One who sees my aimless turning might take me for the
    desert whirlwind:
I am nothing within nothing; if I have any being, it
    comes from you.

While I was your rolling pearl, why did you let me go
    astray?
If my dust is on the mirror of life, it comes from you.

Cupbearer, you have my cup a dawn glow of blood and
    tears;
if I am languorous the morrow of a night of revels, it
    comes from you.

It is with you that Galib takes refuge, great Mevlana:
the cap I wear with pride, it comes from you.

Şeyh Galib

Love is a lamp of God, I am its moth;
love is a shackle, my heart is its crazy captive.

Since becoming a sharer in the secret of your glance
my heart became a friend of the friend, a stranger to
the stranger,

Making no difference between dry piety and endless
carouse—
such is the libertine way of the masters of ecstasy.

The black soil of the reveler's world is full of
abundance,
the sun of wisdom rises in the tavern jar.

He drinks the wine mingled with poison of the glance
of those eyes;
I could be tipsy from the languor of those blue eyes.

Take care, do not neglect that sleeping dagger,
its tale is always the gossip of death.

Galib, enter the secluded palace of pleasure and see its
secret,
the wise way of the daughter of the vine is something
else.

Şeyh Galib

مسقط الراس سمروح وبهاكنت أموج
بلده بوجهه فيها كلَّ شيء و يسروح
وردها من سأسبيل وصخاربها مسروح

A wedding banquet.

Interior of a harem.

Jewish bride, Iran circa 1846.

Jewish bridegroom, Iran circa 1846.

Hebrew
Poems

War begins like a pretty girl
with whom every man wants to flirt
and ends like an ugly old woman
whose visitors suffer and weep.

Samuel ha-Nagid

Man's wisdom is in his writing
his mind at the tip of his pen
with his pen he can reach as high
as a king with his scepter.

Samuel ha-Nagid

Red in aspect, sweet in taste
poured in Spain, famed in India
faint in the cup, but raised to the head
wine holds sway over heads that bow.
The mourner mingling blood and tears
finds his sorrows melted by the blood of the grape
friends passing the cup from hand to hand
seem like gamblers dicing for a precious stone.

Samuel ha-Nagid

She said: Be glad that God has brought you
to the age of fifty in your life—she did not know
that for me my days that have passed
are the same as the days of Noah of which I am told
I have no time in the world but the time in which I am
and that lasts a moment and passes like a cloud.

Samuel ha-Nagid

My thoughts questioned me, astounded:
To whom do you run like the lofty spheres?
To the God of my life, the passion of my desires
for whom my soul and my flesh are yearning.
My joy and my portion and my creator.
When I remember Him, I am troubled.
Can my song give any comfort to my soul
unless it bless the name of the Lord God?

Shelomo ibn Gabirol

Before I was, Thy mercy came to me,
inverting void and being Thou madest me to be.
Who wrought my image, poured my essence
into the crucible and gave me shape?
Who breathed a soul in me
opened the belly of Sheol and took me out?
Who led me from childhood until here?
Who taught me to understand, caused me to marvel?
Indeed I am clay in Thy hand.
Thou didst make me, in truth, not I myself.
I shall confess my sins, and not say to Thee
"The serpent deceived me and led me astray."
How can I hide my guilt from Thee? For indeed
before I was, Thy mercy came to me.

Shelomo ibn Gabirol

At dawn I seek Thee
my Rock and my Refuge.
I shall direct my prayer to Thee
morning and evening.

Before Thy greatness
I stand affrighted
for Thine eye sees
all the thoughts of my heart.

What can the heart
and tongue achieve?
What strength has my soul
within my body?

The song of man
is pleasing to Thee.
Therefore I praise Thee
while still God's spirit is in me.

Shelomo ibn Gabirol

Come to me at dawn, my beloved, and go with me,
for my soul thirsts to see the sons of my people.
For thee I shall lay golden couches in my chamber
I shall spread for thee a table, I shall make ready for thee
    my bread
I shall fill for thee a bowl, from the clusters of my
    vineyard—
Drink to thy heart's delight, may my taste be pleasing to
    thee
for with thee I shall rejoice, as the scion of my people
the son of thy servant Jesse, the prince of Bethlehem.

Shelomo ibn Gabirol

Rise and open the door that is shut,
and send to me the roe that fled.
The day of his coming he shall lie all night between my
    breasts
there his good smell shall rest upon me."

"How looks thy beloved, O lovely bride,
that thou sayest to me 'Take him and send him!'
Is he beautiful, ruddy, and goodly to look on?"

"That is my beloved and my friend! Rise and anoint
    him!"

Shelomo ibn Gabirol

My heart is in the East, and I am at the end of the
  West—
How can I taste what I eat, how can it be sweet to me?
How can I fulfil my vow of pilgrimage, while yet
Zion is in Frankish bonds, and I am in Arab chains.
I hold it light to leave all the bounty of Spain,
as I hold it dear to see the dust of the ruined sanctuary.

Yehuda Halevi

On Arriving As an Uninvited Guest

I was not called but merely chanced to call.
Amid your numbers I shall not be found.
If I am missing I shall not be missed
If I attend I shall not be attended.

Yehuda Halevi

Jerusalem

Place of beauty, delight of the world, city of a great
    king,
for thee my soul yearns from the limit of the West.
The murmur of my compassion is quickened when I
    remember ancient days,
thy sanctity that is exiled, thy sanctuary that is desolate.
Oh, that I had an eagle's wings,
to water thy dust with my tears, and make it sweet.
I have sought thee, though thy king is not in thee, and
    in the place
of thy balm of Gilead there is a snake, a serpent and a
    scorpion—
Shall I not cherish the very stones, and kiss them?
And the taste of thy clods will be sweeter to me than
    honey.

Yehuda Halevi

One grey hair appeared on my head
I plucked it out with my hand.
It answered me: "You have prevailed against me alone—
What will you do when my army comes after me?"

Yehuda Halevi

Ofra washes her clothes in the waters
of my tears
and spreads them to dry in the sun
of her radiance.
With my two eyes, she needs no spring,
with her beauty—no sun.

Yehuda Halevi

Darling one, you have made me captive with your
    loveliness
and burdened me with great toil in this captivity.
For since the day when parting came between us
I have found no likeness of your beauty—
So I refresh myself with a red apple—
its smell is like the myrrh of your brow and lips
its shape like your breast, and its color
like the red of your cheek.

Yehuda Halevi

I go early to the great man's house—
They say: he has gone riding.
I call on him at evening—
They say: he has gone to sleep.
Either he mounts his horse or mounts his bed.
Alas, for a poor man, born without a star.

Abraham ibn Ezra

The Muslims sing of love and of passion
the Christians of war and revenge
the Greeks of wisdom and devices
the Indians of parables and riddles
and the Israelites—songs and praises to the Lord of
   Hosts.

Abraham ibn Ezra

The sphere and signs all went awry
the day that I was born.
Were I to deal in candles
the sun would not set until I die.

I strive to prosper but I cannot
for my stars have thwarted me.
Were I to trade in shrouds
none would die as long as I lived.

Abraham ibn Ezra

On a Man in a Large Turban, of 200 Cubits

A turban bound on the head of a lout—
I thought it a vessel full of shame.
It was very big, standing on emptiness
like the sum of existence suspended over the void.

Yehuda al-Harizi

Absconding Patron

Offspring of meanness, brother of gripe and stint
in whom all niggard qualities are assembled—
I praised his name in two languages
going astray in word and utterance.
But when I sought him I did not find him
They told me he had gone to Harran.
Though he has hidden himself from me
he has left his bad name in the slit of my pen—
like a mouse that runs into a hole and leaves
its tail in the mouth of the cat.

Yehuda al-Harizi

She said—seeking to leave me when she saw that my
    hair was shot with white—
"Dawn has risen on your head, I am a moon, dawn
    banishes my radiance."
"Not so," I answered, "but a sun, you shine by day, if
    but you do not hide."
She said: "You have no more strength to chase after
    love; what will it profit you if I stay?"
"I am as fierce as a lion to do your will," I said, "nothing
    is changed in me but my appearance."

Todros ben Yehuda Abuʾl-ʿAfiya

From Prison

Dear birds, fly to our friends,
carry greetings from sufferers who sit immured in a
    dungeon.
Tell them we are hungry and thirsty, but
we eat the bread of tears and draw the blood of the
    heart.
We sit in a dungeon, dark and low, as if aborted,
amid fleas and gnats and avid lice we lie
and little beasts that have not yet a name
pulsate like lovers at the time of passion.
Here the fly buzzes at the bee, and the rat
bares his teeth, and together they lie in wait for body
    and soul.
The jailers are swift to oppress, and the guards
have orders to bring no bread—so too even the ravens.*

Todros ben Yehuda Abu'l-ʿAfiya

---

*A reference to the Biblical account of how the ravens brought
food to Elijah (1 Kings 17:4–6).

ABOUT THE POETS

Abraham ibn Ezra (ca. 1090–1167), of Toledo, Hebrew poet, philologist and commentator, author of important writings on Hebrew grammar as well as many poems on a wide variety of topics, both sacred and profane. He was greatly admired both for his wit and his learning, and may be the original of Robert Browning's "Rabbi ben Ezra".

Abu'l-ʿAlāʾ al-Maʿarrī (973–1057), was born and died in the Syrian town of Maʿarrat al-Nuʿmān. Blind from childhood, his powers of memory enabled him to acquire immense learning, and to produce many books. Some are works of scholarship, especially philology and rhetoric; others reflect his quality as a thinker and poet. One of his works, an account of a visit to heaven and hell and of conversations with their inhabitants, is said to have inspired Dante's *Divine Comedy*.

Abu'l-ʿAtāhiya (748–825) Born in Kufa in Iraq, of a humble family. As a child, we are told, he sold pottery wares in the streets. His inborn poetic gift gave him access first to literary and then to governing circles. His fresh and unconventional style is attributed by his admirers to his natural gifts and spontaneity, by his detractors to his humble origins and limited education. At a certain stage he seems to have undergone a religious experience, and became a pioneer of religious and didactic poetry in Arabic. His simple, direct language won him great popularity, and many of his verses were set to music and performed.

Abū Nuwās (ca. 747–813), born in Ahwāz, went to Iraq as a young man and lived first in Basra, then in Kufa, finally in Baghdad. He became one of the most famous poets of his day, and made a career at the courts of the Caliph Hārūn al-Rashīd and his successor al-Amīn. His poetry is witty, elegant, versatile, and uninhibited, including wine songs, hunting songs, satires, and love poetry both straight and gay.

Anvarī (d.? 1191) born in Abīvard in Khurāsān, died in retirement in Balkh, a master of panegyric and elegy who worked at the court of the Seljuk sultans. A famous quatrain of Jāmī names him, along with Firdawsī and Saʿdī, as one of the "three apostles" of Persian poetry. His poems include a number of short, sometimes pungent pieces, reflecting different aspects and events of his life at court. According to some literary historians, he also practiced as an astrologer, and his career in both capacities came to an end when he predicted a devastating gale which failed to occur. Put to shame, we are told, the poet ended his career and spent the rest of his life in seclusion in Balkh.

Al-Aʿshā (before 570–after 625), the pen name of Maymun ibn Qays, was born and died in an oasis south of Riyād. During his lifetime however, he traveled extensively, probably as a merchant. In one of his poems, he tells how "to make money, I traveled round the world: Oman, Homs and Jerusalem" as well as Ethiopia, Iraq, Iran, and southern Arabia. His pen name, al-Aʿshā, means "dim-sighted," and at some stage he became completely blind. He continued however to practice his poetic art and earned his living by writing panegyrics.

ʿAṭṭār (ca. 1145–1221), Persian mystical and allegorical poet. Born in Nīshāpūr, he lived for a while in Mashhad, and then traveled widely in the lands of Islam, apparently as a wandering dervish. Later he returned to Nīshāpūr and practiced as an apothecary (whence his pen name: ʿAṭṭār, a druggist or perfumer), at the same time composing Sufi poetry. He seems to have led a quiet life and, unlike many other Sufi poets, did not travel but stayed at home. He was killed in a massacre during the Mongol attack on Nīshāpūr in April 1221.

Bākī (1526–1600), Ottoman poet and panegyrist, served Sultan Suleyman the Magnificent and several of his successors. Born in Istanbul, the son of a muezzin, he started as an apprentice saddler, but by hard work, study, and talent won the attention of a circle of poets and eventually, by means of an ode to Sultan Suleyman on his victorious return from Persia, of the court. He is said to be the greatest of Turkish lyric poets.

Bashshār ibn Burd (ca. 714–784), of Basra in Iraq. The son of a bricklayer of Iranian origin, he is reckoned the first of the many Arabic poets of non-Arab extraction. He is said to have been blind from birth and extremely ugly, but these disabilities did not prevent him from having a remarkable career both as a courtier and as a lover. His life spanned the overthrow of the Umayyad Caliphs and the accession of the ʿAbbasids, and he found patrons among both. A complex and versatile figure, his love poetry is marked by realism, clarity, and the frequent use of dialogue.

Daqīqī (ca. 932–ca. 976), Persian poet. On the basis of one line (see pg. 100, last line) he is said by some to have been a Zoroastrian, but the linking of the faith with music, wine and debauchery, all forbidden by Islam, suggests that this is no more than a literary conceit. He is credited with having begun the composition of the great Iranian epic, the *Shāhnāme,* or *Book of Kings,* but was murdered by a slave when he had written only a thousand verses. The epic was completed by Firdawsī. His surviving poems include panegyrics and poems on love and wine, wisdom, and nature.

Farazdaq (ca. 640–ca. 728), literally "lump of dough," the pen name of Tammām ibn Ghālib, a tribal poet famous both for panegyric and satire. He was born in eastern Arabia and lived most of his life in Iraq. Many stories are related of his dealings with his various patrons, his adventurous life, and his skill in invective.

Farrūkhī (d. 1037) a native of Sistan and a poet at the court of the celebrated Sultan Maḥmūd of Ghazna. He is said to have sung his poems and accompanied himself on the lute.

Fuzūlī (?1480–?1556), Turkish poet, was born in Iraq and lived most of his life in Baghdad. He wrote in Persian and Arabic as well as in his native Turkish. In the preface that he wrote to his own collected poems, Fuzūlī describes how his life was consecrated to literature and especially to poetry. He appeals to his readers not to despise him because of his provincial birth and regional dialect. His appeal was heard. Though his language is Azeri Turkish, he was esteemed by the Ottomans, who first conquered Iraq in 1534, as one of their greatest poets.

Gālib Dede (1757–1799), also known as Şeyh Gālib, regarded as the last major poet in the classical Ottoman tradition. He was born in Istanbul, the son of a government official who also, it is said, played the kettledrum at a neighboring Mevlevi (Islamic mystical order) convent. At first he tried, like his father, to combine a career in government service with the spiritual life of a Mevlevi dervish. Before long however he was unable to maintain this double life, and devoted himself entirely to the Mevlevi order, eventually becoming sheikh of the famous and venerated Mevlevi convent in the Galata district of Istanbul. His poetry had already made him known to Sultan Selim III, a lover of poetry and an admirer of poets. His patronage took the form of restoring Mevlevi convents, and commissioning a superb manuscript copy of Ghālib's collected poems. The gilding alone, we are told, cost three hundred gold pieces. His poetic works consist of a divan, and an allegory entitled "Beauty and Love."

Ḥāfiẓ (ca. 1325–ca. 1390), Persian lyrical poet, was born and lived most of his life in Shiraz. He is said to have been born to a poor but literate family and have worked, among other things, as a baker's apprentice and a manuscript copyist. He earned his soubriquet, Ḥāfiẓ, literally memorizer, by learning the entire text of the Qurʾān by heart. He enjoyed only intermittent favor at court, and seems not to have shared the material advantages of his panegyrist colleagues. He is considered one of the greatest of Sufi poets, though his songs of love and wine sometimes convey more of reality than of allegory. In one of his most famous lines, he says that for the mole on his beloved's cheek he would give Samarqand and Bokhara. Legend has it that the great Sultan Tamerlane, who added Shiraz to his domains in 1387, summoned the poet and angrily asked "By what right do you pretend to give away my cities?" To which the poet replied: "Yes, indeed, and it is by such acts of reckless profligacy that I have reduced myself to my present state of penury." The Sultan, according to the story, took the hint and made a suitable cash donation.

Al- Ḥallāj (857–922), literally the wool carder. An Arabic writer of Persian origin, author of mystical works in both prose and verse. He was born in the Iranian province of Fars, probably the son of a wool carder, and moved to Iraq, where he applied himself to religious and more particularly Sufi studies. It is said of him that he took only one wife, and that they stayed together all their lives. His preaching, however, aroused the hostility of the orthodox, and he was accused of charlatanry, sorcery, blasphemy, and finally apostasy. He was condemned by a council of theologians and, after nine years imprisonment in Baghdad, was put to death.

Ibn al-ʿArabī (1165–1240), was born in Murcia in Spain, to a family that traced its origins back to pre-Islamic Arabia. When he was eight years old, his family moved to Seville where he began his formal education. When he was still young, a vision during an illness led him to the mystic way. He traveled extensively in Spain, North Africa, and the Middle East, and finally settled in Damascus, where he spent the last ten years of his life. One of the greatest and by far the most prolific of Sufi writers, in both prose and verse, his influence on later mystical literature in Arabic, Persian, and Turkish was immense, and may even have extended to Christian Europe.

Ibn al-Muʿtazz (861–908), ʿAbbasid prince and poet, author of a work on Arabic poetics and of very innovative poetry, both in form and in content. In December 908 a group of discontented officers and officials plotted to proclaim him caliph. He agreed, on condition that there be no bloodshed. The plotters duly proclaimed him as caliph, but abandoned him when the palace guards opposed his appointment. "The caliph of one day" as he came to be known, took refuge in the house of a jeweler, but was found and strangled.

Ibn Quzmān (d. 1160), an Arabic poet from a distinguished family of poets and scholars in Cordova. What little is known of his life portrays him as a heavy drinker and reckless bohemian constantly short of money and in need of patronage. He is especially admired for his use of the *zajal,* a popular verse form composed in the Arabic dialect of Spain.

Ibn Sahl al-Andalusī (1212–1251), also known as al-Isrāʾīlī, a native of Seville and a convert from Judaism to Islam, whence his soubriquet. In the usage of the time, Yahūdī denoted Jewish faith; the more respectful Isrāʾīlī denoted Jewish origins. He left Seville when it was captured by the Christians in 1248 and settled in Ceuta, on the northern coast of Morocco, where he entered the service of the governor. He was drowned in a shipwreck while on a diplomatic mission for his master. His work consists largely of love poems, including a number of early poems dedicated to someone called Mūsā, and later poems dedicated to another called Muhammad. Some critics have conjectured that these names might be metaphors for his early Judaism (Mūsā is the Arabic form of Moses) and his final embrace of Islam. Others see them simply as the objects of his affections.

Ibn Zaydūn (1003–1070), was born in Cordova to an aristocratic Arab family. In the course of a somewhat checkered official career, there were times when he enjoyed high favor, and served various rulers in the capacity of vizier and of ambassador. He is regarded as the greatest of the Arabic poets of Spain. Many stories are told of his long and stormy relationship with the poetess Wallāda, daughter of the caliph of Cordova. Best known for his love poems, Ibn Zaydūn also wrote prose, notably letters.

Jalāluddīn Rūmī (1207–1273), the most famous of all mystical poets in the Persian language. He was born in Balkh, now in Afghanistan, and after many travels finally settled in Konya in Anatolia, then known to the Muslims as Rūm—whence his pen name. Among his followers he came to be known as *Mawlānā,* Turkish pronunciation *Mevlâna,* our Master. He founded an order of dervishes known after him as Mevlevi, and sometimes, among Westerners, as the dancing or whirl-

ing dervishes. His long, mystical poems are among the mas-
terpieces of Persian literature. He also wrote some verses in
Turkish, the main Muslim language of Anatolia, and even a
few in Greek.

Jamāluddīn Mohammad Isfāhānī (d. 1192) spent all his life in his
native city of Isfahan. He worked as a panegyrist for the
great families of the city, and for the last Seljuq sultans of
Iraq. He was also known as a painter and a goldsmith.

Kamāluddīn Ismaʿīl Isfāhānī (ca. 1172–1237), said to be the last
great Isfahānī poet of the old school. The son of Jamālud-
dīn, he succeeded his father when still a teenager and won
esteem and protection by his panegyrics and elegies. In ad-
dition to his work as a panegyrist, he also celebrated the de-
lights of physical as well as mystical love and wine, in qua-
trains and other forms of verse. He was killed by the
Mongols when they sacked Isfahan.

Al-Khansāʾ (ca. 575–ca. 640) Ancient Arabian poetess, chiefly re-
membered for her elegies on her two brothers, killed in the
wars of pagan Arabia, and her four sons, killed fighting in
the cause of Islam. Her poetry well expresses ancient Ara-
bian notions of honor and glory.

Khāqānī (1126–1199), born to a simple artisan family in Shīr-
vān, near Baku, now in the Republic of Azerbaijan, and spent
much of his life in Tabriz. His father was a carpenter; his
mother a Nestorian Christian converted to Islam. He was a
noted Persian poet in his day. Besides the usual panegyrics
by which he earned his livelihood, he also composed mysti-
cal poems and quatrains. A spell in jail for offending his pa-
tron, allegedly by a display of spiritual pride, provided the
occasion for his famous prison ode.

Köroğlu (16th century), literally the "son of the blind man," the
hero of a cycle of popular stories and romances, portraying

him as a rebel, a bandit, a defender of the poor and aveng-
er of the wronged. The stories rest on a genuine historical
personage who is known from contemporary documents
to have been active in the region of Bolu, in Turkey, in
1580–82.

Mehmed II, (1432–1481), known as *Fātiḥ,* the Conqueror, Otto-
man sultan, who conquered Constantinople in 1453. Like
many of the sultans, he was an occasional poet.

Mihri Hatun (d. 1506), that is, Lady Mihri, the daughter of a kadi
(judge) who was also a poet. She spent most of her life in
and near Amasya, in Anatolia, and was a member of the lit-
erary circle of Prince Ahmed, the son of Sultan Bayezid II.
The Ottoman literary tradition relates that she fell in love
many times but insists that all these loves were chaste and in-
nocent, and that she led a life of unremitting virtue. Her
poems reveal a good literary education, but at the same time
retain remarkable freshness and simplicity. One of the ob-
jects of her affections was a certain Iskender Çelebi, son of
the famous Sinan pasha. Though described as both beautiful
and ardent, she remained unmarried.

Mihyār al-Daylamī (d. 1037), a convert from Zoroastrianism to
Islam, who composed poetry in Arabic reflecting both his Is-
lamic faith and his pride in his Persian identity. Originating
in Daylam, in northern Iran, he appears to have lived in
Baghdad. He was converted and instructed by a well-known
Shiʿite poet and descendant of the Prophet, whom he
revered and whose death he lamented in a famous elegy.
Some Sunni literary historians, condemning his choice of
the Shīʿa form of Islam, observe that his conversion only
switched him from one corner of Hell to another, but all ad-
mire the beauty of his Arabic poetry.

Mujīr (d. ca. 1197), Persian poet, a pupil of Khāqānī.

Al-Mutanabbī (915–965), literally "one who pretends to be a prophet," the soubriquet of Abu'l-Ṭayyib Aḥmad al-Juʿfī, regarded by the Arabs as one of their greatest poets. Said to have been of humble origin, he was educated in Kufa and then prepared for a career as a poet by living among the Bedouin in order to learn their pure and elegant Arabic. After leading an adventurous life, he served for some years as a professional panegyrist to various rulers, notably to Sayf al-Dawla in Aleppo and the Nubian eunuch Kāfūr, the ruler of Egypt. Finding this distasteful, he switched from panegyric to invective and fled to Iraq.

Nedīm (d. 1730), Ottoman poet. Born the son of a Kadi in Istanbul, he made his career as a scholar, and served as a judge, college professor, and as the librarian of the Grand Vizier Ibrahim Pasha. He perished, along with his master, during a Janissary mutiny. Many of his poems are panegyrics to the Sultan and the Grand Vizier. He is better known for his lyrical poems, remarkable for their elegance, their light touch, and the joy of life that they reflect. Many of his poems were set to music and sung.

Nesīmī (d. 1417), Turkish Sufi poet, a follower of the Hurūfī school of mystics. A native of Iraq, he is said to have composed poems in Arabic, Persian, and Turkish, of which the last-named are the most esteemed. His mystical musings sometimes went beyond the limits of strict orthodoxy, and in 1417 he was flayed alive in Aleppo, in accordance with a *fatwa* from the Mufti of that city. His biographer tells this story. In denouncing and condemning him, the Mufti cried out: "He is unclean! His death is unclean! If any one drop of his blood touches any limb, that limb must be cut off!" Just then a drop of Nesīmī's blood spurted, fell on the Mufti's finger, and stained it red. An elderly Sufi saw this and said "In accordance with your own fatwa, O Mufti, your finger must now be cut off." "No" replied the Mufti, "it fell while I was citing an example, so no legal consequence follows." The dying poet extemporized this couplet: "If you want to cut one finger of the zealot he turns and flees from the truth / See this poor devotee who when they flay him head to foot still does not cry out."

Niẓāmī (ca. 1140–6—ca. 1202–17) little is known about his life, perhaps because he was not a court poet. He was born in Ganja, now in the Republic of Azerbaijan, where he spent most or all of his life. By common consent he ranks as one of the greatest Persian poets. His most important work consists of his five narrative poems, including one on Alexander, known in Arabic, Persian, and Turkish as Iskandar or Iskender. Another deals with the famous love story of Khusraw and Shīrīn. His style is epic, but he is concerned with the amorous and emotional problems of his heroes as well as with their warlike exploits.

Nuṣayb ibn Rabāḥ (d. 726), born in an oasis between Mecca and Medina. He was of slave birth, probably African, and grew up discharging menial duties among the Bedouin. His command of Arabic and his poetic gifts won the attention of the Umayyad prince ʿAbd al-ʿAzīz ibn Marwān, who bought him from his Bedouin masters, set him free, and became his patron. He appears to have resided mainly in Medina, with visits to Egypt and to Syria, where he worked as a panegyrist. He is also the author of some more personal and, in a sense, autobiographical poems.

ʿOmar Khayyām (d.1132), Persian poet and scientist. Among his countrymen he was chiefly known for his work in mathematics, physics, and calendar reform. His quatrains (*rubāʿiy-yāt*), dashed off in odd moments, survived in various manuscript versions, but did not become famous until they were translated into English verse by Edward Fitzgerald (first edition 1859, second and definitive edition 1868). More than a thousand quatrains are attributed to Khayyām; scholarly research has accepted only a small proportion of them as authentic. They have, however, brought him a fame that has almost totally eclipsed his life's work as a scientist.

Rābiʿa al-ʿAdawiyya (d. 801) of Basra, greatly admired for her devout and mystical poetry celebrating the love of God. She became famous in her lifetime and a legend thereafter, inspiring several biographies and even two films. She is said to have been born into a poor family, and to have been stolen as a child and sold as a slave. But her manifest holiness won her freedom, and she withdrew to a life of celibacy, at first in seclusion in the desert, then in Basra, where she gathered a circle of disciples. According to an early source, she was asked: "Why don't you ask your kinsmen to buy you a servant to discharge your household tasks?" To which she replied: "By God! I would be ashamed to ask worldly things from Him to whom the world belongs. How can I ask it of those to whom it does not belong?"

Rūdagī (d. 940), Persian poet, singer, and musician, regarded as the first great classical poet of Iran. According to his biographers, he was born in Rudak, a suburb of Samarqand in the present-day Republic of Uzbekistan. He was born blind or became blind at an early age. He is said to have composed a great number of poems—one historian gives the figure as 180,000—and assembled them in a collection (divan). Unfortunately, the divan has not survived, and his poetry is known only from many single verses cited by Persian lexicographers, and some complete poems preserved by anthologists and quoted by historians. They reveal a court poet who enjoyed the pleasures of life, to which he gave direct and natural expression. According to a well-known story, his patron Prince Naṣr of Bokhara so relished the delights of his vacation in Herat that his courtiers became homesick for Bokhara, and begged him to return, but without success. Rūdagī then composed and declaimed a poem describing the beauties of Bokhara and the pangs of homesickness to such good effect that the Prince, we are told, leapt on his horse and rode off to Bokhara without waiting to put on his boots.

Saʿdī (ca. 1213–19–1292) born and died in Shiraz, but is said to have traveled extensively for some thirty years in various parts of the Islamic world. He is regarded by the Iranians as one of their very greatest poets, and his books became and have remained staples of Persian education. His most famous books are the *Būstān (Garden)*, completed in 1257, and the *Gulistān (Rose Garden)*, completed in the following year. Both books are collections of moral and didactic tales. The first is entirely in verse; the second in mixed prose and verse. He also wrote love lyrics, mystical poetry, and, of course, panegyrics in honor of the rulers of Shiraz. Saʿdī is almost certainly the first Persian author to be translated into European languages. A translation of the *Gulistān* into German was published in 1654, followed by other European languages. The *Būstān* was translated into English by the Oxford Orientalist Thomas Hyde (d. 1702).

Sanāʾī (d. 1131), Persian court poet and mystic. Born the son of a teacher in Ghazna, now in Afghanistan, he spent most of his life there and, for a while, in Marw. After beginning a career as a panegyrist, he abandoned the court and became a mystic. He is esteemed as a pioneer of Sufi poetry.

Samuel ha-Nagid (993–1056), statesman and military commander in the service of the Muslim ruler of Granada, he was one of the first Hebrew poets to compose poetry on secular themes, and especially on politics and war.

Shelomo ibn Gabirol (ca. 1021–1058), one of the outstanding Hebrew poets of the Middle Ages, was born in Málaga and lived most of his short life in Saragossa as a sickly, impoverished orphan. He survived thanks to a Jewish courtier, who appreciated and encouraged his talents. He composed both worldly and religious poetry, the latter both devotional and mystical.

Suḥaym (d. 660), literally "little black," the pseudonym of a poet also known as "the slave of the Banūʾl-Ḥashās," the name of the family that owned him. Born in Ethiopia, he was brought to Medina as a child. The poems attributed to him deal with love and race, often interrelated.

Todros ben Yehuda Abuʾl-ʿĀfiya (1247–ca.1305), Hebrew poet of Toledo, who worked as a panegyrist for a prominent Jewish family of Navarre. He is the author of a number of works in verse and in rhymed prose.

ʿUbayd-i Zākānī (1300–1371), born in Qazvīn to a family said to be of Arab origin, lived most of his life in Shiraz. He wrote mainly in Persian, occasionally in Arabic, both prose and verse. He is most admired for his humorous and more especially his satirical writings.

ʿUmar ibn Abī Rabīʿa, (644–ca. 720), born to a wealthy family of the tribe of Quraysh in Mecca, where he spent most of his life. He is regarded as one of the greatest of Arab love poets. He served for a while as governor of Yemen, and is said to have achieved martyrdom by dying in a shipwreck while on his way to fight in a holy war. He is more commonly remembered as a martyr of love.

ʿUmar ibn al-Fāriḍ (1181–1235), Egyptian poet, famous for his saintly life and his poems of mystical love. Already during his lifetime he was venerated as a holy man. According to an early narrative, the ruler of Egypt, al-Malik al-Kāmil, nephew of the great Saladin, wished to call on him in person, but the poet refused both his visit and his gift.

Waḍḍāḥ al-Yaman (d.? 709), literally "the lustrous one of the Yemen." The poet known by that name appears to have come from the Yemen and settled in Syria, where he served as a panegyrist to the Caliph al-Walīd I (reg. 705–719). He is said to have been put to death by order of the Caliph, who suspected him of being his wife's lover. A number of love poems, relating to this and other affairs, are attributed to him.

Al-Walīd II (d. 744), Umayyad caliph, reigned briefly in Damascus 743–44, remembered as a man of culture and a poet of love and wine. His reign and life were cut short by a revolt in 744.

Yaḥyā of Tashlija (d. 1575), Ottoman soldier and poet. An Albanian from Kosovo, he was recruited into the Ottoman service, and made a successful career. He retained proud memories of his homeland to which he gave poetic expression.

Yehuda ha-Levi, usually transcribed as Halevi, (ca. 1080–1140), Jewish philosopher and Hebrew poet. He was probably born in Toledo and lived most of his life in Cordova. His poetry deals with both secular and religious themes, the latter including his famous poems expressing his love of Zion. This love took him on a journey to the East, where he met his death.

Yehuda al-Ḥarīzī (ca. 1170–1230), poet and translator, the last major writer of the classical Hebrew tradition in Spain. He translated a number of Arabic books into Hebrew, including a commentary by Maimonides, at the request of the Jewish community of Marseilles. There was a market among European Jews for translations from Arabic, which they did not know, into Hebrew, which they did, and al-Ḥarīzī was able to make a career of his work as translator and writer. He traveled extensively in the East, where he also did well as a panegyrist and litterateur. His poems deal with a wide range of topics—love, wine, eulogy, and humor, as well as didactic and devotional poetry.

Yūnus Emre (d ? 1320), Turkish Sufi poet, generally accepted as the first major literary figure in Turkish Anatolia. A mystic, probably a dervish, he is claimed by the Bektashi order as one of their own. Many poems are attributed to him, of which a fair number are considered authentic.

APPENDIX

To GIVE the reader some idea of the rhythms and tonalities in the original, I have appended the texts of four quatrains, one from each of the four languages. The Turkish poem is given in the standard modern Turkish orthography, which replaced the Arabic script in 1928; the other three are transcribed, two from the Arabic, one from the Hebrew script.

I

Lā talqa illā bi-laylin man tuwāṣiluhu
faʾash-shamsu nammāmatun waʾl-laylu qawwādu
Kam ʿāshiqin wa-ẓalāmuʾl-layli yasturuhu
lāqa aḥibbatahu waʾn-nāsu ruqqādu,

II

Yak dast bi-muṣḥaf va-digar dast bi-jām
gah nazd-i ḥalāl mānda gah nazd-i ḥarām
māʾīm dar īn ʿālam napukhta khām
na kāfir-i muṭlaq na musulmān tamām

III

Eğer desem ki havâlar açıldı geldi bahâr
Murâd odur ki benimle mahabbet eyledi yâr
Ya söylesem ki çemen goncelerle zeynoldu
Odur garaz ki tebessümle söyledi dildâr

IV

Ofrā tĕkhabbēs et begādeha bĕ-mē
dim'ī ve-tishtāḥēm lĕ-shemesh zohārāh
Lo shā'alāh mē hā'ăyānōt—'im shĕtē
'Aynay, vĕlō shemesh—lĕ-yōfī to'ārāh

NOTE ON
TRANSCRIPTION

Turkish names and terms are given the
spelling officially adopted when Turkey
abandoned the Arabic script in 1928. Arabic
Persian and Hebrew are transcribed
according to systems in common use.
Diacritical marks are used only in the
biographical notes.

SOURCE NOTES

A FEW of these translations have already been published: in volumes in honor or in memory of scholarly colleagues (1–5), in specialist periodicals (6–10), and in three anthologies (11–13).

1. *Studi in Onore di Francesco Gabrieli* (Rome, 1984).

2. *Fahir Iz Armağanı (Essays presented to Fahir Iz)* (Cambridge, Mass., 1990).

3. *Yādnāma: in memoria di Alessandro Bausani,* vol. ii (Rome, 1991).

4. *Zafarnāme: Memorial Volume of Felix Tauer* (Prague, 1996).

5. *Studies in Honour of Clifford Edmund Bosworth,* vol. ii (Leiden, 2000).

6. *The Afrasian,* 1968 (London).

7. *TR,* 1, 3, 1975–1976 (London).

8. *Edebiyat,* I / 2, 1976 (Philadelphia).

9. *Critical Enquiry,* 12, 1985 (Chicago).

10. *Journal of Ottoman Studies,* 7–8, 1988 (Istanbul).

11. *Eos: An Enquiry into the Theme of Lovers' Meetings and Partings at Dawn in Poetry,* ed. Arthur T. Hatto (The Hague, 1965).

12. *An Anthology of Turkish Literature,* ed. Kemal Silay (Bloomington, Ind., 1996).

13. *A Middle East Mosaic: Fragments of Life, Letters and History,* ed. Bernard Lewis (New York, 2000).

ILLUSTRATION CREDITS

Frontispiece: A picture taken by the royal photographer at the feast described in my opening paragraph. The figures shown are the author / translator with Prince Hasan, the late King's younger brother on his left, and a Bedouin chief on his right.

FROM THE FIRESTONE LIBRARY AT PRINCETON UNIVERSITY
(pp. 81–88):

A-1–3. From Manuscript 62 G; a manuscript of the *Divan* of Hafiz, copied in 926 / 1520, folios 2b, 132b, 133a.

A-4–6. From Ms. 77 G; a manuscript of the Romances of Nizami, dated 846–9 / 1453–5, fols. 76a, 144a, 191a.

A-7–8. From Ms. 79 G; another manuscript of Nizami, dated 970 / 1562, fols. 1b and 313b.

FROM THE TOPKAPI PALACE MUSEUM, ISTANBUL
(pp. 135–44):

B-1. H 986, a manuscript of the *Divan* of Hafiz.

B-2. From H 761, from a manuscript of the *Khamsa* of Nizami, dated 1461.

B-3. From R 1021, from a manuscript of the *Khamsa* of Amir Khusrau, completed in Baghdad in 1463.

B-4. H 1230, fol. 121a, from a manuscript of the *Jāmiᶜ al-Siyar,* dating from the end of the sixteenth, beginning of the seventeenth century.

B-5. H 1230, *Jāmiᶜ al-Siyar.*

B-6. H 802, a manuscript of the eastern Turkish poet Nevai, dated 937/1530–31

B-7. From Album H 2137, probably painted circa 1610.

B-8. B 408, fol. 19a, album of Ahmed I, seventeenth century.

B-9. From H 1010, 56a, a manuscript of the *Divan* of Hafiz.

B-10. Topkapı Palace Picture Gallery.

B-11. Topkapı Palace Picture Gallery, circa 1710–1720.

FROM OTHER SOURCES (pp. 171–74):

C-1. Manuscript 23, page 205, in the Oriental Institute of the Academy of Sciences in Leningrad. From the *Maqāmāt* of al-Hariri, a well-known Arabic classic. The manuscript was apparently made in Baghdad, circa 1225–1235.

C-2. An etching by an early nineteenth century English artist, Thomas Allom.

C-3a&b. In the private possession of Professor Myriam Ayalon, in Jerusalem. The inscriptions are in Judaeo-Persian, that is, Persian in Hebrew letters.

28 DAYS